Fashion design

Fashion design

Joanne Brogden

Studio Vista: London
Van Nostrand Reinhold Company:
New York

A Studio Vista/Van Nostrand Reinhold Paperback
Edited by John Lewis
© Joanne Brogden 1971
All rights reserved. No part of this work covered by the copyrights hereon may be reproduced or used in any form or by any means – graphic, electronic or mechanical, including photocopying, recording, taping or information storage and retrieval systems – without written permission from the publisher.
Published in London by Studio Vista Limited
Blue Star House, Highgate Hill, London N19
and in New York by Van Nostrand Reinhold Publishing Company
a Division of Litton Educational Publishing, Inc.
450 West 33 Street, New York, NY 10001
Library of Congress Catalog Card Number: 72–136746
Set in 10/11 pt Baskerville
Printed and bound in the Netherlands
by Drukkerij Reclame N.V., Gouda
British SBN paperback 289 79837 x
                 hardback   289 79838 8

CONTENTS

Author's note 5
1. The great fashion designers 7
2. Training: conception, perception and realization 41
3. Sources of ideas 66
4. Occasion and function 74
5. Style and styles 79
6. Haute couture; boutique; ready-to-wear 84
7. The profession 89

AUTHOR'S NOTE

A knowledge of the various ramifications of the world of fashion is as important as knowing how to draw your first roughs, or cut your first toile.

This book attempts, within its limits, to introduce anyone who has had some visual training, and who has a real interest in fashion design, to the practical aspects of design and into the depths of this fascinating trade.

It is quite obvious that one cannot learn the art of fashion design by reading one short book. What is attempted here is to sketch in the kind of world in which the fashion designer works.

Marie Antoinette dressed in the style of Rose Bertin, 1784 by Vigée Le-Brun. *Château de Versailles*

Chapter 1   THE GREAT FASHION DESIGNERS

Fashion design is an idiosyncratic occupation. The great and original fashion designers have followed many different lines. There is much to be learnt from a critical look at just how they came to the trade and developed their own particular flairs.

For many centuries high fashion has emanated from the wealthy and leisured classes. But the origin of the term fashion design as we know it started with a highly influential milliner called Rose Bertin round about 1770. Although for many years previously women had prepared clothing and trimmings for various customers, this was against the laws in France until the late seventeenth century. Only men were legally permitted to be recognized clothing purveyors to ladies of society. A petition was presented to Louis XIV in 1675 at the time of the great influence of Madame de Maintenon, asking that women dressmakers should be allowed to make petticoats, skirts and peignoirs; and stating that it would accord with propriety, chastity and modesty that ladies should be dressed by members of their own sex. This appeal to modesty was accepted and the petition was successful.

C. F. Worth, an Englishman, is accredited with being the first couturier to inaugurate a system similar to that which has been in use ever since. Most of the great designers, whatever their nationality, have been in business in Paris, and one therefore gets the impression that all good designers have been French. But Worth, Redfern and Molyneux were English; Schiaparelli and Valentino are Italian; Dessès a Greek; Balenciaga a Spaniard; Mainbocher an American. The truth is that the Parisian has always had a particularly strong feeling for apparel and decoration. With earlier social systems and close affiliation with the remarkable courts of the kings of France, the most entertaining pastimes were clothing and intrigue. And the seeking out of perfection in all designed objects was obsessive among the French. This encouraged highly skilled craftsmen to work in Paris. The fact that such craftsmen were within call has given the designers a great advantage.

The Great Fashion Designers are primarily chosen in this book because they were innovators. This chapter is devoted to those who consistently made an impact on the world of fashion or who radically changed the whole outlook towards clothing.

Portrait of Rose Bertin, c 1780

ROSE BERTIN

The earliest known dressmaker of influence is Rose Bertin, although naturally the system had supported names before, dressmakers such as Mme Labille, who had a shop where *articles de la mode* could be purchased, such as ribbons, flowers, gloves and trimmings.

Rose Bertin worked originally in a small *merchande* in Abbeville, her home town, and from there went to Paris to the House of Pagelle. Designing at that time merely consisted of placing the right kind of flowers and ribbons on a more or less basic silk garment. But Bertin had a high critical sense and an eye for proportion; she was heard by members of the aristocracy to comment strongly on these points. Rose was fortunate enough to be financed by the Duchesse de Chartres, and a house was opened for her in 1773 in the Rue St Honoré. She rapidly became the adviser and *consultante* for Marie Antoinette and was even known as the Minister of Fashion. Having reached and kept to the top of her profession for some years, when the Revolution came she was obliged to flee from Paris. In 1792, after the arrest of Louis XVI and Marie Antoinette, she went to Germany. She travelled with stuffs and work-girls in search of the good business available during the time of the German emperor's coronation. She also opened a shop in London,

Pauline Borghese (sister of Napoleon) wearing a Leroy dress, from a painting by David, 1804

where *émigrés* delighted in her company and work. But funds were low and the ill winds were blowing for poor Rose Bertin who, even at the height of her influence and fame, was often not paid for her work. Finally, when she returned to Paris in 1800, she found herself ousted from the smart scene; other fashionable, perhaps more topical, designers had taken her place and she herself died in 1812, in obscure poverty.

LOUIS LEROY

The next designer one might consider important is Louis Leroy. Born in 1763 and brought up in the atmosphere of the Paris Opéra, where his father worked, he soon began to show a specific interest in ladies' clothing. He of course was affected by the Revolution, as he had been working for the aristocracy, but luckily he was asked by the Convention to design suitable dresses and clothing for the New Régime, and found favour with his highly patriotic work. He was in fact an established designer when Rose Bertin returned to Paris. His forte was Grecian-style robes, but which (to comfort a few of his older clients returning from exile) were decorated with a deal of ribbons and embroideries. Although his business was going well, he had to resort to trickery and bribery to obtain the favour of the Empress Josephine. He at length succeeded and received the final accolade when he made up the designs for her coronation. Leroy ran his establishment very much as the grand couturiers of a century and a quarter later. He sold accessories and perfume as well as the clothes he designed. Leroy worked on as a couturier for the Empress Marie-Louise of Austria, Napoleon's wife after he had divorced Josephine. Eventually, when Leroy was older, he gave over his establishment to a niece. He died in 1829. Some of his designs and clothes can still be seen at the Musée Malmaison.

WORTH

Charles Frederick Worth was an English designer who influenced the entire fashion world of Paris and even of Europe. A poor boy from Lincolnshire, he was born in 1825 and at eleven years old had to begin work to help support his family. After some time he went to London, still at a very tender age, and joined the staff of the draper's firm of Swan and

Charles Frederick Worth, c 1880

Edgar, as a fabric salesman. Apparently he greatly enjoyed this work. Some years later, having learned the rudiments of running a business (at Swan and Edgar he had been made a cashier), he decided to go to France. He worked in a draper's shop in Paris for a year, at the same time learning to speak French. He next found a situation in a most chic fabric shop called Gagelin in the Rue de Richelieu, where many years before both Bertin and Leroy had had premises. Women then virtually had all the power as dressmakers. It took some years of slow progress for Worth, while still at the fabric house of Gagelin, finally to be allowed to open within the firm a dressmaking establishment. Eventually Worth found a backer, a Swede named Otto Bobergh, and premises were taken in the Rue de la Paix, above which Worth and his French wife lived. The House of Worth was the first nineteenth century fashion house to

Evening cloak by the House of Worth, from *Gazette du Bon-Ton*, 1914

use models or mannequins to show the clothes. Worth became the first designer to hold the monopoly of dressing the wealthy European aristocrats and royalty for a consistently long period. He is said to have invented the crinoline and after that the bustle. He also introduced to the French the English 'tailor-made' for women. The crinoline was used expressly to disguise the fact that Eugénie was pregnant, and naturally what Royalty wore was immediately followed by all the court and society women.

Worth is highly important, as he was an instigator of new fashion on many levels. Apart from his undoubted creative ability, he was the first fashion designer to run his concern as a real business. From this he made vast amounts of money, so that the firm was able to continue for many years after his death. He died in 1894 and his sons Jean and Gaston continued the business. After their death the sons of Gaston Worth, Jean and Jacques, carried on.

True inventiveness in this firm really died with the original Worth, although the firm exists in London to this day.

PAUL POIRET

Although other fashion houses were flourishing, it was Paul Poiret who was the next great influence in the world of fashion. His conceptions were at that time utterly revolutionary and shattered the complacency of the period.

Born in relatively humble circumstances at Billancourt, at an early age he showed a precocious interest in women's apparel. Against his family's wishes, he spent two years training, first at the famous house of Doucet, and then at Worth. His arrogant and forceful behaviour forced him to leave both positions, although it was evident that this young man had talent.

When he finally opened his own establishment, the impact was tremendous. Poiret was responsible for freeing the hitherto monstrously restricted, prow-like bosom, by inventing the *soutien-gorge* (the first effort at a brassière); but he proceeded to hobble the legs and ankles. Otherwise his designs tended to be supple and languid.

Although there was an underlying simplicity either in decoration or

Poiret clothes drawn by Georges Lepape from *Les Choses de Paul Poiret*, 1912

Paul Poiret, c 1928

shape, his clothes showed a strong feeling for the exotic, in their tendency towards oriental influences. This influence had simultaneously hit the arts, the theatre and the interior decoration of houses. Like Balenciaga in recent times, Poiret showed great aptitude for dotting his 'i's with fabulous hats, often smallish in size, but with marvellously juxtaposed plumes thrust through the hat like great brushes, in contrast to the lean body shape.

Paul Poiret cultivated and made use of the talents of various artists, for business purposes and out of friendship. His association with Georges Lepape, whose drawings have crystallized this epoch, has left a marvellous documentation of his fashion work in the book *Les Choses de Paul Poiret*, and in Vogel's magazine *Bon-Ton*. Both Dufy and Matisse worked on ideas for textile prints for Poiret. Vlaminck and Segonzac were personal friends of his. Poiret belonged to the world of Diaghilev, Bakst and Benois.

With his tremendous zest for luxury and extravagance, Paul Poiret forcefully exerted his influence, particularly with the *demi-mondaines*. He dressed the last great European courtesans, at the fabulous dream house on the Faubourg St Honoré.

The genteel world of Worth was a far cry from that of Poiret, whose clothes were in total contradiction, being quite unladylike in daring colour, form and decoration.

After the 1920s, Poiret ceased to be an influence on the contemporary smart scene and although he had made a vast amount of money earlier in his career, became almost a pauper, and died penniless, an arrogant eccentric, on the French Riviera.

COCO CHANEL

The most remarkable thing about Chanel is that she made a comeback and became once again a *succès fou* after fifteen years absence from the fashion scene. She gave up the fashion business in 1939 while she still had a very smart establishment. This was not solely because of the war. She had made a great amount of money during the thirties. Her collection of jewels was legendary. In the fifties and sixties she proceeded after two coolly received collections in 1954, to make a lot more money and an increased reputation. Chanel has been a great innovator, changing during the twenties and thirties the entire concept of fashion for the wealthy, using cheap 'worker's' cloths instead of sumptuous Lyons materials. Through her clothes she changed the image of the smartly dressed woman, turning her into an insolent little gamine who wore easy clothes and was the very antithesis of the *grande dame*.

Gabrielle Chanel was from the Auvergne, supposedly from a poor family. She has told varying stories of her origins. She started with a hat shop in Deauville in 1914, eventually reaching Paris. Everything she did carried her feeling for understatement; in the colours she used – black, beige, grey, and white with navy; and even the casual way in which jewelry was to be worn. It is said that all her ideas for junk jewelry were based on her own fine jewels and she loved to mix up her pearls, emeralds and rubies and wear them on skinny jersey dresses – made from the kind of sandy-coloured wool like old men's vests. Her style has always been throw-away.

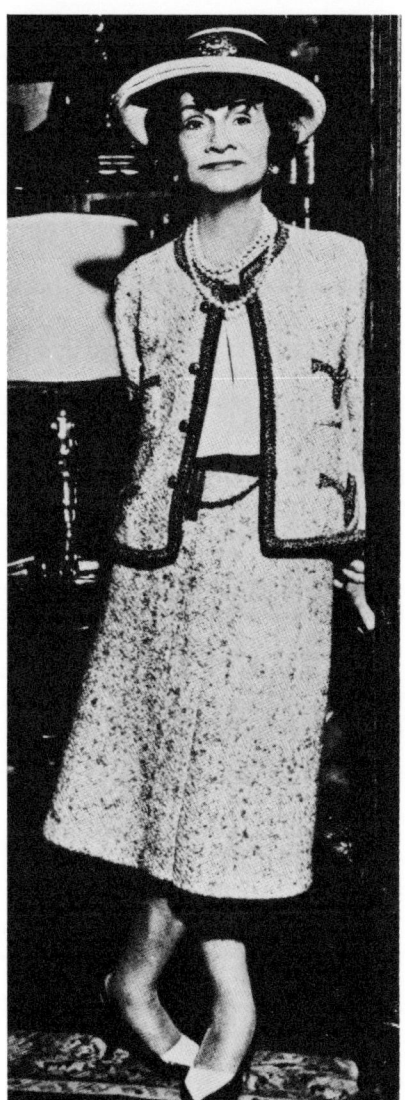

Jersey suit by Chanel, 1934

Mademoiselle Chanel, 1957

Chanel's clothes during the overlap period with Poiret were a complete antithesis of Poiret's ideas. While his showed flamboyant arrogance, hers showed an understated and simple arrogance; usually in 'nothing' colours – but always free and supple. On her courageous re-opening in an entirely new epoch, the clothes Chanel designed were still based on a principle of suppleness and easy wear. After a period of rather rigidly constructed clothing in the manner of Dior, Fath and Balenciaga, Chanel's suits and coats, for instance, seemed light as feathers, since no building was used – no hard canvases or stiffening. Soft English Linton tweeds, but trimmed almost excessively with gold fancy buttons, silk facings and cuffs, intricate braid edgings, perhaps fabric and lining stitched through together as in quilting. No-one has ever used such a mass of detail with such infallible taste and success. It was her pale wool suits which put out of fashion the wearing of formal cocktail dresses. Having twice powerfully influenced the world of fashion, Chanel is doubly great. Her consistency was part of her strength: she adhered to the same simple concept and the same basic philosophy.

Madame Vionnet, c 1955

MADELEINE VIONNET

Vionnet and Chanel epitomize the twenties and thirties. Chanel with her casual philosophy, and Vionnet because of her fantastic knowledge of cut and construction which brought forth the conscious using and designing of the bias and cross cut. This has had a most remarkable influence ever since and is one of the primary principles, whether in fashion or not, of dressmaking. Mme Vionnet was not renowned for being a colourist and, as did Chanel at that time, advocated nondescript tones.

Vionnet was born in Abbeville. Her origins were modest, like those of so many designers in fashion. When twelve years old she began work in dressmaking and at twenty went to London, after some time at Vincent, a dress house in the Rue de la Paix. On returning to Paris, she obtained work at a very well known house – that of Callot Sœurs, owned by three sisters. One of these sisters, Mme Gerber, was the designer, and Vionnet cut toiles for her. In 1907 there was an opportunity for Vionnet to design at Doucet (where Poiret had worked) and after causing a furore by uncorseting her models, she had much success. Only after that did she open her own house, in her own name, having learned her trade and having given much in return. Up till the early thirties hers had been modest success but then she moved to the Avenue Montaigne, now the centre for couturiers. The business was large and there were 1200 employees. Vionnet by this time had established a very rich clientele, who adored the severity and classicism of her clothes, the quality which had upset Doucet so much in the earlier days.

Her philosophy was that clothes should be made in a suitable fabric and not stiffened into shapes which were not inherent to its nature; and that the female anatomy was all important and was to be followed and utilized, not disguised or grotesquely contorted. She would never allow padding and rarely resorted to trimmings (superfluous). In one sense she was a sculptor. The famous business closed in 1939–40.

Vionnet's cross-cut evening pyjama in silk crêpe, 1934

SCHIAPARELLI

Schiaparelli was in complete contrast to the designers of the thirties. The employment of foreign *émigrés* to knit fancy sweaters was the beginning of Schiaparelli as a designer. She did not commence with any traditional training of cutting and sewing. A volatile Italian, from a cultivated family, she showed her talents as a designer of surrealist ideas. Comic, aggressive and often vulgar, many of her designs were sheer novelty and not at all in the grand tradition of French couture.

However, they did amuse and delight many wealthy women who were ready for a change. The word Shock is synonymous with Schiaparelli and indeed she was responsible for a perfume and a shade of pink called Shocking.

Like Poiret, Schiaparelli evoked robust vulgarity, but at the same time she was an innovator of many exciting ideas. She was the surrealist in the haute couture, fond of using curious and possibly unsuitable motifs in her clothes, such as a shoe for a hat, etc. She even employed the painter Salvador Dali to design the window displays in her house on the Place Vendôme, and also used Vertes, Picasso and Christian Bérard to design prints and cloth ideas.

There was rarely any subtlety in anything she did, only studied effect and a wilful contempt of accepted 'good taste'. Strident colour was also a hallmark of this designer.

Schiaparelli's clothes certainly did defy good taste, balance and tradition; and they were possibly a forecast of the chaos to come with the second world war. She was the designer to cater for the hard, smart, amusing type of woman of the mid and late thirties. Her philosophy for fashion might have been the more eccentric, the more chic.

After the war Schiaparelli's inventiveness seemed to weaken. Although several collections were based for instance on themes like animal or insect shapes, on the whole they had little impact. The need to express the qualities, prevalent in the late thirties, of chaos or non-order had vanished and so had Schiaparelli's flair as an influential designer.

Two restrained designs by Schiaparelli, 1934 and 1938

Christian Dior, c 1956

DIOR

After the decade of Schiaparelli's decline, there arose a new phenomenon. His name was Christian Dior, and he became more publicized than any designer before him.

Born in Normandy of a comfortable middle-class family, he was a man of great refinement of taste. Having set up an art gallery which failed, he decided during the thirties and forties to design or sketch hats for Piguet and the paper *Le Figaro,* and then to design clothes. These he succeeded in selling and finally, in need of regular income, he found a job at Lelong in 1942, as did other subsequently famous designers such as Cardin and Balmain. His circle of friends included painters, musicians and composers, young and unknown. Balmain has described Dior as aloof, quiet and modest, even remote, when they worked together at Lelong.

After the second world war, Paris seemed to revive miraculously and soon became the centre of artistic innovation, with ideas popping up like fireworks, despite the four years of deadening occupation. And by 1947 an astounding revolution occurred in the history of fashion, revitalizing the world of clothing – the New Look. This was the name born out of Dior's first collection at his own house. Gentle hints had been given to this new conception of clothing in other designers' previous collections, but it was this virtually unknown designer who, with an immense coherence and clear sight, made a total commitment to it. His designs were the exact opposite of the mass of clothing at that time, utterly luxurious in fabulous fabric and yards of it, complete formality and restriction. The clothes were immensely stimulating, particularly with young people who had never known such qualities in their lives of wartime deprivation.

For each collection during the fifties, there would be a publicized signature – the H line, the A line, the Y line, etc. And indeed this designer was responsible each season for inventing new shapes and new cuts. Yet very seldom were they as eccentric as the initials infer. His ideal woman was utterly feminine, in contrast to Balenciaga's.

Dior was always associated with tremendous luxury, of introverted quality, with particularly ravishing painterly colour schemes, fabulous

A New Look coat by Dior, 1947

cloths and exquisite bullion embroideries.

Always in the vast collections, which were a manufacturer's dream for wealth of ideas, there would be several types of women catered for. The refined, the understated, the girlish, the pretty, the Junoesque, the cocotte: all within the same idiom but revealing different characters. He died just before the difficult and dangerous first ten years of success was up, and remains a legend of inventiveness and taste. His influence resounded throughout the world for many reasons, not only for the New Look, but for the many subsequent collections he produced.

Dior's philosophy appeared to be that women should ravish the eyes of the beholder and advertise their extreme femininity, even when dressed casually.

The house of Dior continued after his death, with Yves St Laurent and later Marc Bohan as designers.

Balenciaga, c 1950

BALENCIAGA

Christobal Balenciaga, although a fashion king concurrently with Dior, had entirely different ideas of what was chic. Very hard and severe, very rigorous and starkly simple, his tailoring was utterly immaculate and completely architectural. He was the tailor-designer *par excellence*. He built a name and a style on total exclusiveness, on monumental design quality, on high prices and a great reluctance for any personal publicity. No concessions were ever made on any of these points. Commercialization was of no interest to him.

A Basque from Spain, Balenciaga at an early age began to dressmake in his small village, but made his first essay into professional dressmaking in San Sebastian. In 1936, already about forty years old, he found enough capital to open in Paris – the only place for the serious designer. The premises he took were on the Avenue Georges V; he remained there until he gave up his business in 1969.

In retrospect, Balenciaga's clothes appear never to have been influenced by any other contemporary designer. His attitudes towards the making and designing of fashionable clothes were strongly Spanish and based on classic rules. He never used the seasons to change line or detail; any minute change would take place almost imperceptibly over a length of time. The words sombre and brilliant apply to both style and colour, which latter he used with electrifying daring, sureness and skill, particularly in evening wear.

The clothes of Balenciaga specifically suited severe, plain women; women whose attraction lay in hard chic, and whose beliefs matched his, in that refinement lay in the constant principles of classicism.

A typical coat shape by Balenciaga, 1953

André Courrèges, 1970

ANDRÉ COURRÈGES

Balenciaga had a group of disciples, young men who worked for him, who were to become famous. They were Courrèges, Feraud, Ungaro and Venet.

Courrèges broke away from the house and on first starting his own business showed clothes that owed much in style and conception to his previous employer. If one wanted a Balenciaga look at a less expensive price, one went to Courrèges.

This changed completely in 1963 when he showed a startlingly austere collection of day clothes made in heavy double gaberdines but using light sugar almond colour and white.

What he showed were trouser suits of immaculate construction which had for that period of time a certain tough look; and very short dresses of utterly simple shape but again beautifully constructed and using no darts. Courrèges even showed glittery silver trousers, baring the navel, though worn with a long split coat for evening wear.

These clothes showed a new and refreshing concept, apparently utterly modern, and were the beginning of the space-age cult in clothing. The simple hard little dresses were worn with his famous white boots and essentially suited an Amazon type of girl, active and striding on long straight legs.

Courrèges was the universal hero. The clothes were supposed to be functional (they were not) practical and elegant (practical – no; elegant – yes), but they were 'pilots', that is to say, they heralded the beginning of a new era in women's clothing. That collection, and those immediately following, had an immense impact which lasted until 1968. Subsequent collections showed an obsession with novelty, but not true innovation. A hard basic look in hard modern fabric decorated with novel detail has been superseded by the softer influence of Yves St Laurent.

An early Courrèges suit, after Balenciaga, 1962

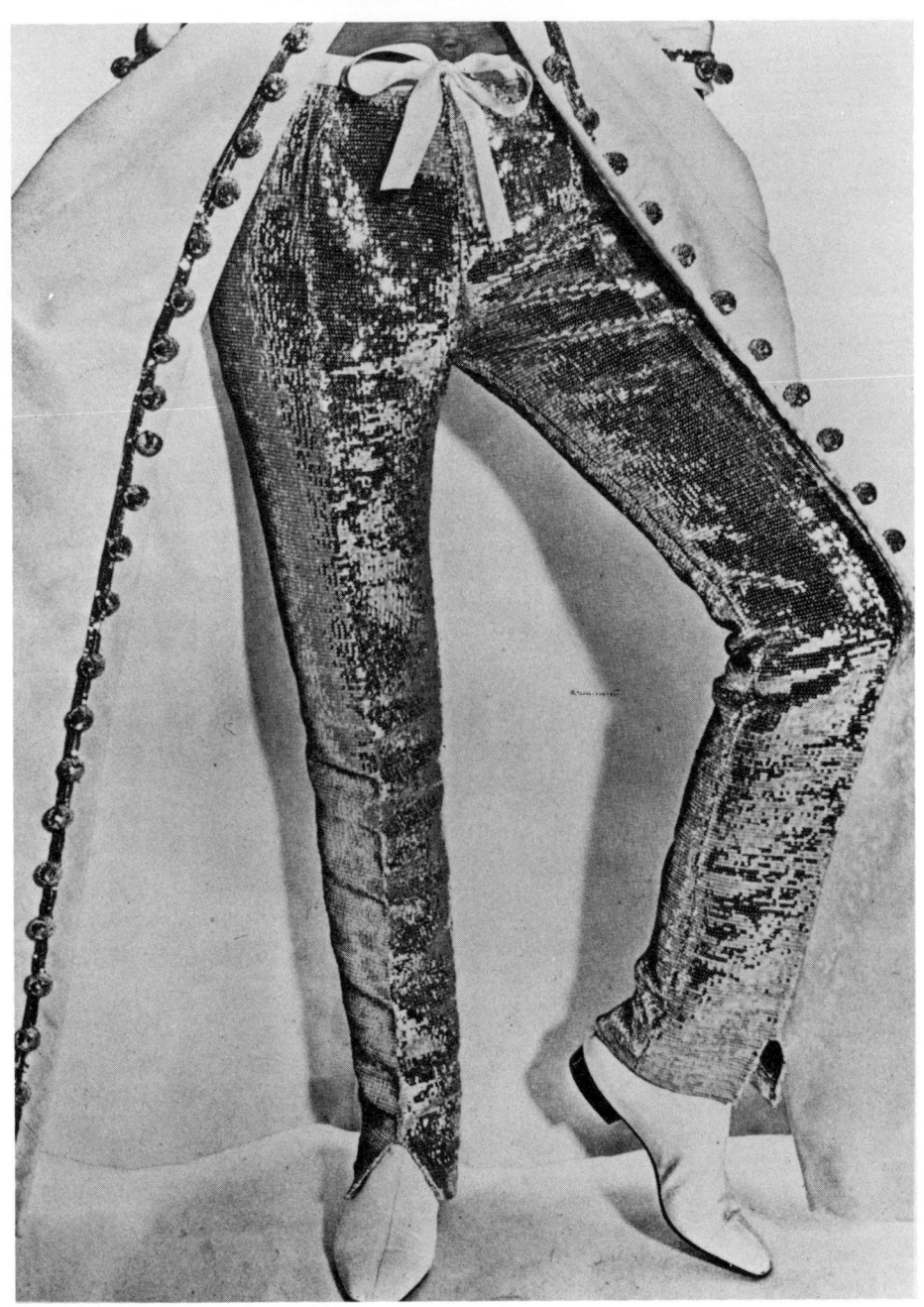

The Courrèges idiom of 1964

An early St Laurent dress in the sophisticated manner, 1962

Yves St Laurent, 1970

YVES ST LAURENT

St Laurent studied at the Chambre Syndicale School of Fashion in Paris, and it was through an International Wool Secretariat competition that Christian Dior saw, and liked, his designs.

In 1957 it was first realized that Dior had a new assistant, and ten months after the death of the master St Laurent was publicly presented to the world as the successor.

His first collection was an enormous success, well publicized and well received by international buyers and fashion press alike. But the Dior machine was not to the liking of the new young designer, even though he had produced collections of clothes well within the handwriting of the house. St Laurent's third collection showed signs of his own individuality breaking out. Short in length, young and insolent, influenced by the Blousons Noirs, they were clothes which still showed their impact in 1969. It was the beginning of the fashion revolution of the sixties. The collection was not a commercial success; buyers did not see their elegant lady customers in clothes suggestive of toughness and the smart young could not afford the high prices.

Previously the House of Dior had secured deferment from military service for St Laurent, as he was in effect a national asset. But following this flop collection he was by coincidence directed into the army. There followed a nervous collapse.

It was through friends that St Laurent found an American backer called J. Mack Robinson and after a two-year lapse St Laurent was back in the fashion scene, setting up in a private house on the Rue Spontini, some way from the accepted fashion house area.

The first collection showed his Rajah clothes, indicating a revival of oriental influence. Though first shown by him in 1963, this style persisted throughout fashion to the end of the decade.

While at first St Laurent designed clothes which showed admiration for sophisticated women, each collection has developed a younger quality or flavour, more reflective of his own society and age group. The trouser suits in jersey, with their safari jacket or battle-dress flavour, were repeated everywhere and almost became a uniform; his pastiche peasant clothes reflected the hippy scene before most people were aware of it. Usually this designer's clothes minimize accepted notions of femininity – his designs are rarely pretty or delicate. For some time he has shown distinctly male influences on women's clothing; for example, the famous velvet smoking suit, the safari jackets and suits.

St Laurent reacts with great sensitivity to situations in the air and his reactions are shown in his designs. He undoubtedly reflected the general feeling of carelessness – almost of anti-fashion – but has always managed to show perfect and well-designed versions.

The softer St Laurent idiom of 1970

MARY QUANT

The name Mary Quant epitomizes the fashion revolution of the sixties. Although not a designer of the couturier class, she has had an enormous influence on the development of the type of design and designer prevalent at the present day. Quant is a name which in the past has been associated with anti-couture fashion and the activities of this English ready-to-wear designer have had repercussions throughout the European and American continents.

Mary Quant's great contribution was that she proved that a young amateur with interest in clothing could break the conventions and restrictions of the fashion trade. Previously it was almost unheard of for anyone so young and inexperienced to set up a business and to succeed so well. In her wake followed many talented young designers of ready-to-wear clothes, expressing no allegiance to Paris decrees and none to the large mass production concerns of the time.

Quant set up her business primarily in the form of a shop in Chelsea called Bazaar, and did not initially design the merchandise. It was only on experiencing great difficulty in finding clothes she felt to be suitable and desirable for girls of her age and inclinations that she began to suggest to a manufacturer that small changes might be made in his existing merchandise. Bazaar became the 'in' shop for fashionable clothes for the young, and from then on Quant began to manufacture her own ideas. At that time her clothes outraged the high professionals, but certainly showed a fresh eye and an appreciation of her market. So began the decade of clothes for the young designed by the young.

But the tremendous success of this venture in ready-to-wear clothing and accessories encouraged every student designer to imagine that they too might succeed, despite inexperience. Thus began the era of non-professionals, willing to take the risks in a trade about which they were completely ignorant.

Boutiques based on Mary Quant's Bazaar sprang up like mushrooms, many of then naturally destined to collapse after a few months. The young British designer look began to have an enormous impact in the world. Names such as Tuffin & Foale, Roger Nelson, Biba, Ossie Clarke became internationally known, but only these and a few other of the

Mary Quant, 1970

strongest designers survive now. Eventually the large business-like concerns found they had to court such designers – or those whose work was in the same idiom.

The clothes of Mary Quant were not necessarily great innovations or inventions in the manner of the highly skilled designers in Paris. Quant's designs for clothes did offer a new freedom of concept about fashion. Even in Paris this encouraged and made noticeable very exciting young ready-to-wear designers such as Michèle Rosier, Sonia Rykiell, Emanuelle Khahn and Daniel Hechter.

One other point of importance is that through Mary Quant's influence, some years previously, designers like Ossie Clarke could be successful and bring about their own special contribution, such as joining with textile designers in a tandem with both receiving equal recognition. In a search for completely original and therefore extra desirable prints for his clothes, Ossie Clark started to use the designs of Celia Birtwell. Her quality of designs for cloth has been emulated everywhere, and she has won widespread recognition as a fabric designer. Rarely in the past have these textile designers received an accolade for their work; that has been reserved for the firms for whom they worked.

It might even be, in the future, that there could be a complete amalgamation in one person of clothes designer and textile designer. Emilio Pucci has already for some years shown the possibility of such a thing with his fantastic prints, completely personalized, on utterly simple silk jersey dresses. But this quality has recently become an ambition of many students. So far the idea has not spread into the less expensive market of ready-to-wear.

The days of the custom-built haute couture as purveyors of expensive clothes for the very rich may well be numbered. The upsurge of young designers brought about by Quant and her successors may be the truer indication of the direction in which the fashion trade is going. The levelling of what was the haute couture into ready-to-wear and thence to mass production seems to comply with world social conditions.

But one point remains and that is, that whatever direction the fashion world takes, designers are always going to be the key figures in this ephemeral business. There is room at the top and on the way up.

Chapter 2 TRAINING: CONCEPTION, PERCEPTION AND
         REALIZATION

Earlier in the century fashion designers would construct clothes for a client and work straight into the cloth, cutting an approximate shape and fitting on the client until they achieved perfection. Nowadays designers for mass production and also the couturiers work differently. They make drawings and then hand them out to their various workrooms or sample rooms for patterns to be cut or toiles to be made up in cheap calico. The latter method is obviously the better one.

The simplest and most convenient way to conceive a design for clothing is to draw it. Communication is achieved much more speedily with a drawing than with words, and professional designers must communicate their ideas to others, whether they are involved in the making-up processes or are potential customers.

TRAINING

The training of a potential designer is a process which takes years, not months. Individual characteristics can still only come to light after years of constant effort. No-one should be frightened of making mistakes. That is the way to learn. Some students will have a natural aptitude for what are termed bread-and-butter clothes, that is, those which are not particularly creative, but which will sell well. A few students will have those extra qualities of imagination and love which will make them innovators of new fashions. They must be flexible in thought. Everyone knows the difference between good, well designed clothes which are difficult to fault, and the clothes which bowl over the spectator with admiration for their magic. The period of real fertility of design ability is said to be little more than ten years for a creative designer. Yet there are exceptions such as Chanel, who seems to keep on designing in a classic manner and yet continues to produce clothes that are always desirable and original.

Much has to be appreciated and learned in the practice of design. There is knowledge of drawing, texture, colour and proportion, and the knowledge of applied detail, of fabric properties and cut. Then there are methods of pattern making, grading the sizes, draping on the stand. The actual manufacture of the clothes, that is the making up, entails knowledge of tailoring and dressmaking, thereby creating an understanding of the cloths to be used. Add to these things the learning of mass production methods and business methods and the curriculum is nearly complete. There is still the understanding of the millinery and accessories that go with each design, although it is usually only as a student that one has to cope with these important subsidiary subjects. By undergoing a thorough total look training, no part of fashion escapes the fashion designer. Having had a little experience of these subjects, the student can then at least select what branch of the industry he or she is most suited for, and indeed may specialize in during the final year of his or her training. Much of what may be taught is theoretical, because of the constant changes in all the ideas and methods of manufacture of articles to do with fashion.

THE BALANCE OF DESIGN AND CONSTRUCTION

Much again depends on the flexibility of the teachers of fashion design, as to whether they are open minded yet critical of all the new things that develop. As a student designer, all the possible things to be used must be constantly in mind. The balance of ideas work (designing) and the technical instruction should be more or less equal. Often the act of trying to create through drawings is more palatable to a young designer than the working out of patterns or indeed the execution of the garment or outfit. This is naturally a slower process, but it is imperative that one should know how to do it all and be able to carry out the construction. So many small problems present themselves in making up that the inexperienced do not foresee. Even the fully fledged designer cannot know how to solve everything. He will still make mistakes.

Perhaps the idea of using some unexpected cloth for a certain design may seem exciting. Already the design may have been produced without difficulty in another fabric, but the drape or handle inherent in a different one will present problems to be sorted out by trial and error. One learns the difficulties of trying to achieve from a flat, possibly unconventional fabric, a three-dimensional shape in which the human body can move easily.

Understanding should be developed about the joys of the unexpected, of clash and contrast, of ignoring any set rules at any given time in fashion. To do this with intelligence, those rules must first be known, then broken. If care is not taken, work will become introvert; in other words it will become so clever from a styling viewpoint as to turn completely inwards and lose all fashion value. That is as dangerous as ignorant over-statement. But this advice is premature for the novice. For them the conventions must be learned, the simple ideas and methods fully understood first. Any item of clothing may be designed, providing that the basic rules are adhered to. In a sense, the first and the final years of such training can be completely contradictory, but at no stage should design work be left uncriticized or not analysed fully, after the statements of ideas have been made. Such criticism will come from professional designers, teachers or even fellow students. Learning to accept intelligent criticism is part of the training, as is sound discussion or argument. You acquire knowledge by asking how and why, not by accepting blindly.

Although the importance of draughtsmanship is strongly advocated in this book, there are some people who are potentially good designers but who will never master this skill. In this case several patterns of drawings should be made, in various poses, and used constantly. Even a basic shape like that of a paper doll can be presented with enormous charm and simultaneously be informative. Indeed the early fashion drawings of Lepape are little more than that, but still give a tremendous aura of the fashion of their time.

ROUGHS: THE FIRST STAGE IN DESIGN

A series of rough ideas can be worked on to produce one final, well thought-out design. These rough ideas will include variations, such as trying to place small details in new but workable positions; or varying shapes and embellishments, or changing the cloth, colour and texture and putting them together with differing methods and techniques. Obviously a critical process of elimination is used. Every designer must start with a brief, or a set problem; such as, for instance, a particular category of clothing governed by price range, age group and function. The drawings and ideas must fit in sensibly with such categories and yet remain fashionable. These sketches are the initial experiments, and

Examples of designer's rough drawings

Fashion drawing by René Bouché, 1959, showing the difference from a designer's drawing

with experience it is possible to eliminate flaws in a design while actually making a drawing.

These drawings are called roughs and can be of any size the designer wishes, although usually fashion designers' roughs will be small, about four or five inches in height, and the finished drawing will be not more than ten inches high. A designer resident with a ready-to-wear firm will hardly ever have either the time or the need to do 'finished' drawings, painted and textured, whereas the free-lance designer will present the brief with colour and texture and the relevant samples of material attached. Neither of these types of drawing is to be confused with the work of the fashion artist, whose job it is to convey an impression, a generalization. Ideally, the drawings of the designer have to be all things to all men, that is, emphasize or generate style, fashion feeling, and at the same time communicate all the information needed for the construction and finish of the clothes. The fashion illustrator, on the other hand, is not required to invent or be knowledgeable of the techniques of making up garments. By the means of his drawing, the designer can also suggest the stance to be adopted and the accessories to be used; both of which are highly important points in the world of fashion. Having evolved with the roughs as many statements in design as possible, the designer's critical faculties really have to get going to select the best solutions to the brief, as well as show the high content of the prevailing fashion. Even the most classic clothes are subject to subtle changes in various details which lose or gain chic from decade to decade. It might be the shape of buckle or buttons; the fact that the buckled belt is roughly tied together instead of neatly buckled, and so on. It is the designer who emphasizes the character – neatness, carelessness, toughness, youthfulness or formality. This character or identity is as important as any seam detail or shattering new shape.

THE IMPORTANCE OF DRAWING

The knowledge acquired through draughtsmanship of the way the body is articulated is itself very useful, and can suggest ideas for clothes. Equally, drawing the way in which cloth hangs or responds can give ideas to a fashion designer. Drawing is essentially 'making a plan of'; a designer is 'a draughtsman who makes plans for manufacture'. This implies that the designer's drawings must be easily read by others and that the three-dimensional object – the garment – must come out exactly as the designer intended, in proportion, detail, character and quality. Of course if one wishes to make very free and loose drawings which perhaps give a real feeling of style, then one should make additional working drawings, i.e. informative diagrams.

There may be several ways in which a certain shape can be achieved, but unless the creator – the designer – suggests the direction to be taken, too much time is consumed in trying out the variations according to the pattern cutter. At the top end of the fashion trade, the couture level, this used to be the method employed. The designer was there to be consulted with due reverence by the *premières* of the workroom. Or indeed, sometimes it was deliberately left to them and to the clever cutters to work out the various possibilities. This method however cannot be used as mass production takes over. Time is money and therefore time must be utilized economically, and the designer who realizes what can and cannot be done within the context of time, skill and labour, will be the successful designer.

In early training a rigorous but intelligent insistence on appreciation of objective drawing is most important. The careful study of the drawings and paintings of such artists as Holbein, Van der Weyden, Van Dyck, Watteau, Boucher and Ingres, can be the means of developing a sensitivity of perception, an understanding of line and form. Artists like these show great economy in putting down an image, and their work is concerned with recording facts and not with self-expression.

It is both unintelligent and futile to copy the current favoured styles of fashion drawing. No originality ever sprang from pursuing anything so ephemeral. Nothing replaces finding out for oneself, and it is preferable to do hard groundwork by studying the work of great painters first-hand and then to evolve one's own methods of drawing.

Eccentric proportions in the drawing of the body can lead to disaster in the made-up garment. Obviously each designer tends to draw his ideal woman wearing his clothes and she is usually a tall, slender woman. But if the height is achieved by drawing legs three times the length of the

Madame Marcotte de Sainte-Marie, 1826. Study by J. D. Ingres showing thorough appreciation of body and garment construction. *Louvre*

Study of a woman seated by Antoine Watteau, expressing the body beneath folds of cloth

trunk (which bears no possible connection to real proportion) or if the shoulders are drawn so narrow that there is no room for suspending a rib cage to hold the vital accoutrements of life, then trouble begins with the literal translation of clothing to fit normal human beings.

The Duchess of Alba by Goya, 1795, showing a somewhat naïve quality of figure representation. Collection Duke of Alba

A woman walking by Hans Holbein, c 1540. Several entirely different cloths are instantly recognizable. *Ashmolean Museum, Oxford*

Katherine Duchess of Suffolk by Hans Holbein, c 1533. Showing refinement and economy of drawing
Reproduced by gracious permission of H.M. The Queen

Madame Ingres (Madeleine Chapelle) by J. D. Ingres, 1814. A deceptively simple drawing indicating a great sense of volume. *Musée Ingres*

At the Theatre by Constantin Guys. A wash drawing illustrating mood.
Albertina Collection, Vienna

Figures of a lady and gentleman by Antoine Watteau. *British Museum*

COLOUR

Colour is emotive and can be particularly so in clothing. For example, a woman wearing a scarlet outfit will create quite a different effect from a woman wearing the same in beige. The line, proportion and detail of a garment are perhaps the most intellectual problems that a designer has to solve. When considering colour, however, the designer must remember that this aspect can exert a curious and powerful influence on personality. Colour is the most emotional and unpredictable feature of design. And a lot of people are colour blind!

There is no such thing as bad colour; it is the misuse of colour, either in juxtaposition or in the nature of the material, that causes bad results. There can be no *new* colours, since every conceivable colour may be seen in nature. The only developments possible are discoveries of new methods of manufacturing pigments and dyes. This is illustrated by the use of chemicals which produce day-glo colour – a term for phosphorescent luminosity. The newness is the effect which reflected light gives to known colour.

When fashion journalists write of new colour, what they mean is that a set of colours, shades or tones have been used together in a manner previously unexplored. The juxtaposition of various colours is one of the skills which convey originality or a fresh approach to colour, as each will affect the other to greater or lesser degree.

All materials used have surface or texture, and it is the degree of absorption or reflection of light upon coloured surfaces which will affect the quality of colour.

The following up of various prescribed colour theories which deal only in flat pigment can never therefore guarantee a good use of colour or even a colour sense. Certainly the use of colour can be learned, but what cannot be taught is the exciting originality of a beautiful colour sense. At the same time as one would respect the fact that yellow, for instance, may appear dominant at one particular time, its use would never preclude the use of other colours to enhance and affect its values. James McNeil Whistler titled a number of his paintings 'Symphony in White'. This did not mean he only used white paint in his pictures. What it did mean was that all the other colours used enhanced the whiteness of the model's dress.

TONE AND SHADE – ANALOGOUS HARMONY

Each pure colour can be broken down into tone and shade, and many degrees of both; it is important that fashion students learn by playing with mixing up colour pigment. It will soon be discovered that the range of greys or blacks is enormous, and the same applies to any other colour. Pastel crayons are probably the best medium for such colour-tone experiments; and since the ranges produced are so comprehensive it is possible that a latent good colour sense may be brought out by the act of selection.

Fashion does undoubtedly affect the popularity of colours, but as with everything else in life, the human eye becomes bored and needs a change. It may be that a colour has become fashionable too quickly and therefore its exclusive quality disappears. Usually of course it is the bright colours, as the extremities in shape, which are the most quickly abandoned. The more excitement one has, the more one needs to get excited; it is something of a vicious circle. This point about colour runs parallel through clothing design and interior decoration. For instance, after the *Belle Epoque,* Poiret introduced bright jewel-like colour with barbaric overtones in contrast to the delicate milky colours prevalent during the Art Nouveau period. He and the advent of the Ballet Russe directed by Diaghilev, tremendously influenced the change in colour and detail, just as Chanel and Syrie Maugham influenced the feeling for beige, white and grey in the early thirties. Later, during the Pop Art phase, bright primary colour and anti-subtlety was the vogue in clothing and interiors of houses, etc. Fashionable clothes and fashionable interior decoration of houses often show the same broad appreciation of certain colour textures and patterns.

It is possible to weigh up colour in the mind's eye so that the value of one small fragment of colour completely unallied to the general and larger amounts of another colour or tone can make a breathtakingly beautiful play in an outfit or indeed in a textile print. It is the scale of one colour juxtaposed with others and literally how much of that particular colour looks well with this or that colour.

The most subtle and beautiful qualities can be achieved by using one colour, but varying the tones of that colour; or one colour and in different textures. For example, shiny black patent or PVC used with gleaming black fur, clerical grey (black) flannel and black surah or shantung. Each one of these blacks will show a completely different quality. This is known as analogous colour. Only skin and hair and make-up will add any other colour.

SHAPE – CUT – FIT

Initially the shape of clothes is governed by the fact that they have to be put on human forms which move and articulate in three dimensions. It is arguable, and a question of personal taste, whether clothes should be comfortable and smart; or uncomfortable and smart. To have one's cake and eat it is surely the cleverest thing to do, though many good designers, usually men, have achieved great success by disregarding a woman's comfort. Oddly enough, most women designers, apart from Schiaparelli, have always designed comfortable and easy clothes. Vionnet, Chanel, Grès, Nina Ricci (and the subsequent designers working for that house) and the American Bonnie Cashin. Of course women designers know the problems and quirks of being female. Countless male fashion students for instance have designed clothes that no woman could ever go to the lavatory in, or indeed get in and out of, in a reasonable amount of time and without being asphyxiated in the process. The fact is that fashionable clothes should, through their cut, fit and manufacture, function easily and smoothly.

It is through cut and the inherent qualities of cloth that shape is achieved. One other factor is underpinning in the form of depressants or stiffeners, on to which the final shape of the garment is built. Cut, that is to say the lines of seaming and darting to make a shape, can be incredibly simple or fantastically complex, depending on what basic shape the flat cloth has to be fitted to. Cut may also be no more than a collection of lines placed together pleasingly or in a novel way, as sheer linear design. There should be no confusion as to the separate meanings of the two words cut and fit, although often a professional will speak of a garment being immaculately cut, and automatically include the word fit, unspoken, in that phrase.

There are three basic forms; straight cut, cross cut and bias cut, all of which are so named because of their relationship to the straight grain of woven fabric. Each has a totally different effect on the behaviour of cloth and again different types of cloth will show a variation in their behaviour. For instance, straight-cut chiffon will hang quite differently from cross-cut chiffon, and these two methods of cutting will obviously affect a fleece coating in quite different ways, as indeed they would organza. Each method and each fabric will give another shape. Equally, if a simple dart shape is made in a soft supple fabric such as crêpe or silk jersey, an extremely gentle shape is achieved, in total contrast to that dart shape being produced in a crisp cotton gaberdine, which will make a sharp and angular shape.

At times when it is considered fashionable to have the body very closely fitted by cloth, clever seaming and cut come to the fore. Nothing but skilful manipulation of fabric can achieve a fit like that of the skin, together with the ability to move. The virtues of jersey are extolled as doing the same job as skin, but to date no jersey or stretch fabric has been able to fit the extraordinary contours of the human female without the aid of shaped seams. Quite simply, it is because large protuberances with subsequent depressions cannot as yet be covered by one single piece of stretch cloth which still retains the same quality, thickness, pattern or colour density as on the flat.

When translating the two-dimensional into the three-dimensional, a designer must consider the relationship of front view to side view to back view. Most of these problems would be solved at paper pattern stage or at least aesthetically at the drawing stage. The movement potential will also have been considered, because ideally clothes should look as good on the move as static.

FUNCTION

This is of paramount importance to designers of sportswear, which should not only show fashion quality and detail but at the same time be totally functional. The strenuous activities of the body in sport necessitate well thought-out garments to cover this mobile frame. The way the limbs articulate in gestures necessary for different sports means that cut cloth must allow for easy moving. Cloth must be chosen with protection, absorbency and elasticity in mind.

The postures needed to play golf or tennis correctly, mean that the designer should understand the activity fully. For instance, tennis is fast and energetic. The limbs dart in every conceivable position and yet elastic cloth would be too hot and uncomfortable. Too loose and flowing clothes would flap about and impede efficiency. A cloth such as cotton jersey would solve these problems and at the time of writing is a fashionable fabric. There must be free leg movement and no restriction at the neck or armhole, otherwise chafing of the skin may occur. This analytical process should work almost unconsciously while one is designing for a specific function of any kind.

ILLUSION

Great care has to be taken if one is trying to create an illusion of narrowness of body, and all proposed details must be well proportioned on a narrow bodice in conjunction with say, collar size and belt size. The area between neck base and waist is really very small and it takes a fine eye for placing much detail successfully within that area. For instance, do the horizontal lines go round the body in a lovely smooth shape? Is the welt pocket the correct size with the half belt at the back, and do they both look good in proportion to the details on the matching coat? Does the collar shape fit in with the depth and angle of the pockets? Even the size of button and style of button must be thought out and judged.

SMALL DETAILS

The points hitherto mentioned have stressed the importance of shape. After this the small details must be attended to, such as method of stitching, topstitching depth, and the number of rows. Or indeed the more inventive kind of detail such as designing a pocket which is totally new, or collars or belts. It may be new yoke shapes, or sleeve shapes or even let-in shapes, or motifs as contrast. The invention might be solely in the unconventional placing of totally conventional detail.

CLOTH

It is imperative that a good fashion designer should have a comprehensive knowledge of cloth. Not of the chemical structure or weave but simply a basic knowledge of the four natural fibres that exist, as well as the man-made. A fashion designer has so many jobs to do and so many problems to work out, that as long as he or she recognizes the handle or behaviour and the suitability to a design, any further technical knowledge of its structure is unnecessary. Technology of cloth has nothing to do with high fashion in clothes. Cloth technology has become so complex with the advent of man-made or synthetic materials that quite frankly it is the prerogative of the chemist, not the fashion designer, to understand the production of cloth from chemical formulae.

ASSESSING A BRIEF

When given a design problem, try and understand the brief and so produce a possible answer which is directly related to the question. Regard the setter of the problem as a client who has to be satisfied. When asked to design for the rich, use expensive or rare materials and methods of making up. At all times include originally designed accessories and ideas for *maquillage* (make-up and hair style). There is fashion in the overall colour and shapes of make-up and hair, even in the way fingernails are shaped and painted. All information and intentions should be clearly made visible, even if later they are to be proved mistaken.

In the matter of the 'how' of designing fashion one can learn only from trial, error, criticism and explanation. There is no magic formula. There are many people who have a great sense of fashion but who could never even be able to start designing.

A SIMPLE DESIGN PROBLEM

It is a good idea to begin designing by starting with a limited objective. For example, design a beautifully simple shirt, with little decoration, in unprinted fabric. What constitutes a beautiful shirt?
1. The material, be it silk, cotton, plastic, wool, or fur
2. The lines and shapes: i.e. seams, yokes, pockets, collar shape cuffs
3. The details – stitching, buttons, length, pleats, tucks, frills
4. Colour and texture
5. The fit and standard of making

Is it to be a casual or informal shirt? A basic shirt, rather like a man's but made in raw silk, of natural colour, but topstitched in brown half an inch from the edges; buttoned with covered silk buttons or beige pearl shirt buttons; one patch pocket; classic shirt collar on stand; long sleeves; classic double or French cuffs to be cuff-linked (with rough-hewn lumps of gold); to be worn casually with gored skirt of raw linen or gaberdine and belted with brown lizard; scarf tucked into neck. That would be the casual way. For formality, unbuttoned, worn with gold and pearl long beads spilling out of the neck, the same rough gold cuff-links and white silk gaberdine skirt or trousers. Details could be listed, and permutations made of them, all within one good basic shirt shape. The same can be done with the accessorizing of this shirt. It is surprising how many dozens of different shirts will come out of this information, using a permutation method.

POINTS OF INTEREST

Only a very few points of interest should be obviously noticeable in one garment or outfit. Otherwise the eye is moving from point to point in an uneasy manner, trying unsuccessfully to correlate all the details. The same rule should be applied to areas of colour, or contrasting textures. If these are evenly distributed, the value of the contrast is destroyed, particularly if the weight of area is identical. In a loose sense, consider the effect of two identical outfits – one a pale top with dark beneath, the other reversed. For some time perhaps convention has decreed that one should wear a dark coat with pale clothes beneath. Just because of this period of time and the eye and mind being conditioned to the habit, it presents no interest; merely reverse the order and the quality is no longer habitual and ordinary. It has become out of the ordinary. The excitement engendered when Christian Dior first produced many years back the first classic raincoat with a mink lining, was colossal: the very notion of cotton proofed gaberdine – a strictly utilitarian piece of clothing which everyone was used to seeing – having as its shock element a delightfully luxurious fur lining. The elegance was heightened when the coat was worn open, in a casual manner, accompanied by lace-up or high-cut shoes. Until then mink had been thought of solely as a status symbol, worn formally with complementary accessories, all of an excessively genteel nature. To connect such material with toughness and carelessness was unheard of, yet one designer did just this, thus showing the very opposite of convention, and so made a new aspect a desirable reality. This also was a good example of making a total look, and this is the factor which marks the difference between a fashion designer and a clothes designer. The designer should know, as a design is made, exactly how the wearing should be, and what the ideal accessories are. Hats, footwear, gloves, bags, belts, scarves and jewelry are very important items for the designer to think about; they complete the total finished look and can pinpoint or accentuate a mood.

PLANNING OUTFITS

A set of clothes which layer, such as sleeveless tunic over trousers and shirt, with matching top coat (perhaps unzipping round the waist to split into skirt shape and bodice jacket) should be planned so that any fragment of the outfit may be dispensed with. What is left should still be workable in a design sense; the balance of colour, texture and details must work well. Always make sure that whatever may be removed to reveal the layer below, blends with or reflects that which is next visible. Clothes should look as attractive in the course of undoing as immaculately closed up, so on undoing the coat or jacket the linings and trimmings harmonize well with the clothes beneath.

Always consider the back view and the sides as well as the front when designing; think of the clothes in three dimensions. Finish off linear detail, as in diagonal and horizontal seam lines. Carry applied pattern on to the back via the sides of the body. Decide what is the most important feature of the design and keep it clear.

ASSESSING FASHION CHANGE

If there is doubt as to the knowledge of a certain change in fashion, be guided by good fashion magazines, or even clothes worn by fashionably dressed celebrities. It may be that several styles are currently favoured; for instance, rough homespun types of clothing, smooth, clingy revealing garments, and hard, slick tailored items may all be fashionable simultaneously. One's own personal preference will be evident and will quite naturally work in any category. Usually a designer will favour a particular style or method within other styles. Learn to cope with various categories for after a while one's real personal talents will be predominant. Be prepared to design in every idiom.

When beginning to learn to design, one must develop an awareness of what constitutes quality and expense; one will then be able to achieve better quality even in inexpensive mass production. As the result of being aware of the handle and sensuality of fine cloth, one can be influenced in the choice of less costly stuffs. Being able to select fabrics which possess a more expensive look than their actual cost is a help towards raising the standard of mass-produced clothes, and greatly affects the appearance of a garment. It is possible to apply this rule to plastics and to fabrics woven from man-made as well as natural fibres. It may be true to say that the more one understands one's manual trade, the better designer one may become. In one or two instances this could be death to creativity, but on the whole much is to be gained from a designer's being able to cut and put together his work.

Ignorance about the cut of clothes, the handle of cloth or the techniques of making up garments can lead a prospective designer into wasteful paths. This is not to say that it is folly to invent new aspects without knowledge of the outcome; but merely to invent at all one must have some knowledge. The waste is in time, endeavour and patience, if not one's own, then that of others.

For example, in designing a flap pocket (which will show a flap on the right side of the garment and a pocket bag on the wrong side), in a sheer fabric such as organdie, it is obvious that all the unsightly construction will be visible through the cloth. The pocket should either be designed to eliminate this, or the pocket bag must be made deliberately visible in a skilful and attractive manner.

Stories about good designers not knowing about the making of clothes are to be viewed with scepticism. While it might just be conceivable in the custom-made clothing trade with the aid of exceptionally clever cutters and seamstresses, it certainly is not possible for professional wholesale designers. Another professional would immediately deduce that the designer was carried by able assistants who had the responsibility of solving every problem, when in fact a well designed sketch should be giving them accurate information. An ignorant designer is in fact no more than a publicity agent.

More and more, with emphasis on mass production, the designer must know how to guide and explain what is wanted and what methods to use. Moreover, with fashion and therefore methods constantly developing, the designer must be flexible in attitude, particularly since materials and machinery are also changing rapidly.

What is needed is thorough concentration at the actual time of producing designs. This means that every grain of knowledge culled and stored in the mind can, when needed, be brought forward and used or described. A basic 'look' which would set the flavour of a series of collections can be a source. A general theme in terms of item or colour can be the source, and after the initial series of roughs is put down, then the polishing and refinement follows. The critical mind and eye selects and rejects by means of reasoning the function and suitability, and then reappraises to make certain that all the magic of an idea still remains and has not been ironed out by that reasoning. It is far better to get down a splendid idea and have to spend a hard time discovering ways to convert it into a three-dimensional one, than to do a design which is easily put through production, but has no presence, no style. Here again – if one knows the bones of one's trade – then other workpeople, cutters and machinists, will respect that, and being confronted with perhaps something quite new and unconventional will listen to instruction on how to handle it. Of course a parallel set-up exists for fabric designers. Knowledge plus imagination and awareness and skills are the key factors. Working to this formula the professionals sort themselves out from the amateurs. The same surely applies to painters, graphic designers, etc. All creators work to a brief, self-imposed or not. Arty inspiration is meaningless.

Chapter 3 SOURCES OF IDEAS

No-one can honestly give a formula for being a good designer of fashionable clothes. The very fact that people are so marvellously varied and in so many ways means that they will appreciate and accept a variety of ideas and visual things. Therefore several tastes will be acceptable at the same time. A good grounding in design and a cultivated taste based on intelligent study of great designers of the past will enable one to move freely through the fluctuations of fashion, and perhaps to create those changes. For instance, after a period of ultra-refined taste one is usually stimulated by an aspect of robustness. Such a swing in taste is desirable; it helps to relieve jaded palates.

By having a sense of history and with the knowledge of many things past, one can behave like a computer digesting and regurgitating, with a personal slant, many ideas. One acquires this knowledge through looking, reading and observing. Observation is more than looking and seeing. A brick is not just one of many rectangular blocks in a building – it has colour, form, texture and density. And one learns to recognize that there are several different qualities in brick as well as in textiles.

SOURCES OF INSPIRATION

People whose job entails the constant giving out of ideas themselves need from time to time some mental stimulation. This can come from seeing the work of other people, or collections of cloth, or collected works of art, or films, or the study of history, or even from travelling. The Victoria and Albert Museum, the Bethnal Green Museum, and the London Museum in London; the Museum of Costume at Bath; the Bibliothèque Nationale and the Centre de Documentation du Costume in Paris; the Metropolitan Museum in New York and most national libraries contain collections of magazines if not clothes; and magazines and journals are most fascinating as the complete panorama of one era is evoked by absorbing from them. The earliest bound copies of journals date from the latter half of the nineteenth century. Before then, dressed dolls and prints were used to carry information about the details of fashionable clothing. These are stimulations from past times, but a designer of clothes might well be influenced by contemporary design ideas outside the field of fashion. For instance, interior decoration, wall-

Basic bodice and sleeve shapes

papers, surface textures, new materials in all industries, architecture, paintings, machinery. Even by seeing unpleasant things and in wishing them pleasant, such reaction can produce ideas.

There is a wealth of detail everywhere which can be very stimulating and set the mind wondering how, why and when. An old book on cutting methods, though interesting, cannot stimulate the imagination quite so strongly, dealing solely in matter-of-fact statements. Fabrics, description of stuffs no longer common or even produced, fastenings, applied design, accessories; these all remind one, or present themselves completely anew, and can generate enthusiasms, around which design ideas start afresh.

A particular type of woman or girl, that is to say, sportive, delicate, sophisticated, gamine, elegant, that one admires can be a source of inspiration or a source of style to a prospective designer. Although it is possible that one's ideal may change several times over the period of a career, this is still a source of ideas. Even the way certain people move about can affect styling of clothes, as a fashion point to emphasize the garments.

THE USE OF REFERENCE

All designers need a reference library. As a start, an informative sketchbook or scrapbook containing every classic or well known type of collar, sleeve, pocket or detail would be of great help to the student designer. The uses of this basic information that all designers need at some time can be endless. It is a beginning from which the more creative will move into originality, and evolve their own inventions and styles. You cannot build on nothing.

Good fashion magazines should be studied carefully, as there is the evidence of other designers' work which will have been influenced by what actually sells, and will probably be in production. At Collection times, which are late January – early February (Spring) and July (Autumn), always ahead of the calendar season, there are reports and photographs and drawings containing information on new styles and ideas. At any time there may be especially commissioned clothes which could be trend-setting. Usually the ready-to-wear merchandise is named and

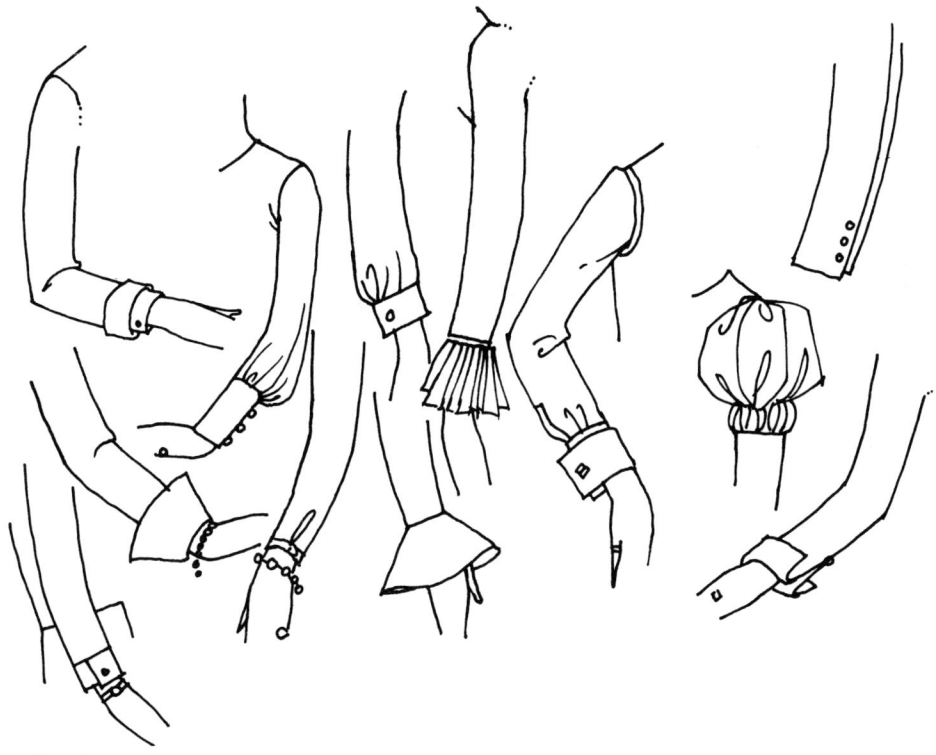

Basic cuff shapes

Basic skirt shapes

Basic collar shapes

priced, together with stockists' names. This information can be a good guide to recognizing the relative cost of the articles, with regard to the type of design. Fabrics are specified and in a photograph one is able to see properties of cloth when made up. And last not least, one can begin to determine the handwriting, the personal qualities and fit them to the name of a firm or designer. Just as a Courrèges design is unmistakable, so is a Jean Muir, or an Ossie Clark.

None of this material is for copying, but simply for stimulation, a reminder of what could be done. 'Could be' is a splendid phrase to help one's powers of invention, probably even better than aimlessly drawing lines on paper.

RAGBAG OR SCRAPBOOK

Every student of fashion design should collect for himself a bag or large scrapbook of samples of fabrics and furs and trimmings. This is the only way to begin to understand cloth, apart from making it up. The average student doesn't make many garments in a year, and then not in a sufficient variety of cloths. Samples of different materials will augment the knowledge one may have and will of course stimulate the imagination. Immediately on touching a Garigue double-face $3/4$-inch fleece, one would know that it would stand by itself, be relatively light, and since it is pure wool it is bound to be warm and to breathe, and that it will make certain shapes without the aid of canvas and interlining. Also, that its very thickness will preclude fussy detail of tiny dimension. The same critical analysis can be applied to velvet, whether it is panne or Lyons; or to crêpe.

There are dozens of different types of cottons, silks and wools, without considering the man-made fibres, which double up on each other. For example, organza (silk) and organdie (cotton). Because of the nature of the basic fibre, the handle and character are quite different. This character is affected by the weave of the cloth as well as the fibre. Similarly velvet (silk), and velveteen (cotton); satin (silk) and sateen (cotton). Crêpe of course can be silk, wool or cotton or man-made, as can jersey, but each of these varieties would have a different handle and usage. This is where a really keen potential designer will show his quality. Just by touching these different stuffs he will instinctively understand how suitable they are to certain designs. Another point is that having to hand a selection of samples, one develops the sense of juxtaposing various textures and colours. The more one thoughtfully plays with these samples, the more one understands just how much versatility exists in cloth and therefore in its use in design. One can achieve the same current look but by using differing cloths of similar character.

There are also masculine cloths and feminine cloths, and colourways and prints. Extremely exciting ideas can evolve from contradicting various laws or reversing the edicts pertinent to one generation or decade in fashion.

Chapter 4 OCCASION AND FUNCTION

Student designers usually start their training blessed with some imagination. This ability has to be disciplined, guided and cultivated to enable workable and suitable clothes to come out of it. Children have on the whole vivid imaginations, but charming as any manifestation of this may be, and logical as it may be for child life, the results are often crude and not very engaging to the intellect. It is a frail quality and quickly diminishes with conventional knowledge. Somehow a good and lively designer has to retain this freshness, while at the same time being bound by the conventions and limitations of production of clothes, with their needs of suitability and function. No-one involved in any field of design can fully justify himself or his work if there is no purchaser to buy them, wearer to wear them, or producer to make them!

Imagination, if not experience, has to come into play, initially to discover the right kind of clothes for certain times and areas, i.e. function. Until the relatively recent breakdown of formal ways of living and behaving, clothes were designed and worn for specific occasions and it was social death to appear clothed in the incorrect garments. During the fifties, cocktail clothes were a recognizable type of dress and every student of fashion, whether they had attended such a function or not, knew exactly what he or she should design. This of course was part of the fashion of living. Who at the end of the following decade, the sixties, ever bothered about cocktail dresses? Style then became much more casual and instead of formal silken dresses, on which to pin one's jewelry with point, it became acceptable to wear, for instance, a casual wool suit in pale tweed. Cocktail parties then passed out of fashion in London, although high dressing still occurs far more in New York, and in the provincial cities of both countries.

As a designer one would have to find out or imagine exactly the fine points of correct dressing for various occasions. One may never have been ski-ing, but it would be quite possible, by observation, to produce good clothes for such a sport, for participant or spectator. Certain evocative words for designers will give enough scope to start their imaginations working, and together with a practical slant of mind, will occasion a much more exciting range of clothes than a highly detailed brief. This could be so tight in specification that it could knock away any imaginative approach. For example, snow – sharp – dry – sun – falling – speed – action – spray – cosy – snug – warmth. One can start immediately. Snow usually indicates cold temperature – therefore warmth is needed. Sunlight means that one can play with colour to get effects. Falling in snow one has to avoid packed snow on fabric melting to become wet. Speed necessitates lightness of stuffs, ease of movement, elasticity of movement in cloth. Ski-ing, unless under battle conditions, invokes a marvellous carefree enjoyment of movement and environment and therefore survival packs are not necessary, neither are handbags or carriers of any other description, but everyone may need to carry something – money, cigarettes, sweets, tickets for ski-lifts, and so pockets are a necessity. These are the practical points brought out of designing to a set of words – providing one knows what the word ski means at all. So as a designer one can immediately conjure up, for instance, a citrus yellow nylon jacket with proofed jersey pants, with cream knitted or fur hat and gloves, and, if money is free, matching ski-boots. A good skier might cope with a muffler. Pockets would be close-fastening, because of the physical stance involved. But above all a sleek outline, on account of speed. It would be totally useless to design very wide trousers open at the ankle, worn with a loose flying-away jacket in open weave or long-haired cloth. Long-haired fur *is* a possibility since fur has more or less wet-proof properties. Naturally these details do not yet begin to include the acceptable fashion or chic points. 'In' groups have their own codes in fashionable clothing as in words or habits. And often seasonable fads start from 'in' group ideas, apart from couturier designers. One has not yet started on the details which would bring such a ski outfit to the point of being really fashionable. Naturally these details must take account of what is currently fashionable.

Anyone can make a list, after being given a few words, of the practical necessities, but what about a non-active occasion – parties or evenings at the theatre?

While designing for a firm one cannot possibly know what each purchaser wants in an outfit for either of these occasions. But everyone is aware of what the current feelings for these may be, and may have some vague idea of the acceptability of a certain garment. Evening wear of one kind or another is the one area of clothing design where impracticability or fantasy is completely acceptable in any epoch. Therefore, the occasion but not necessarily the function is the important guide to the suitability of the design.

This is a particular instance where choice of fabric is governed solely by fashion, not by activity. The value of an intuitive sense of change in fabric fashion is very essential for evening or party wear, as is the choice which shows definition of occasion.

OCCASION

Sportive	active, spectator, in swim, ski, yachting, riding, shooting
Informal	holiday clothes, resort wear, country wear
Daywear	can be formal or informal, lunch in smart restaurant – teaching class full of unruly children
Evening	formal, at home, parties, dances
Wedding	formal or informal participant or spectator

Function and comfort although offshoots of occasion do have different meanings. Clothes which are functional behave properly for specific activities, whereas any other clothes, even when highly fashionable, may be *relatively* comfortable. Any extreme action in normally comfortable clothes could result in tears or splitting of cloth or seams. Ordinary comfort can still be achieved in extreme shape by means of fit and cut. There are periods in the evolution of fashion when comfort has hardly been considered. It is however quite relative to the type of living at certain times. Curiously enough, fashionable females have usually embraced new concepts of fashion as being comfortable. When tight waists and skirts are considered highly fashionable, it seems that the support of *guipières* (elastic belts in corsetry) is comfortable. Conversely, when semi-fitted or slack clothing is admired, the very idea of tight foundation wear is uncomfortable.

What is the function of clothing? It has often been disputed whether it is primarily for protection or for decoration or attraction. The former has nothing really to do with fashion, although much to do with invention. Protective clothing ideas and details are often taken up by fashion designers, who interpret them into points of attraction, e.g. battle jackets, anoraks, use of stuffs, zips and fastenings, bush jackets, boots, plimsolls, skin diving suits, siren suits, dungarees.

The virtues of attraction are what? In leisured societies people consider adornment either to please themselves, to attract others or to display wealth and status. To appear attractive to others is for many people psychologically important. To be well and fashionably dressed embraces certain admired looks, nearly always studied and worked for. A careless look can be more carefully considered and planned than a so-called well-groomed air.

These aspects show that a person is communicating to others and is aware of social codes. The careful preparation of self-presentation to the world shows a consideration for the enjoyment of others. Naturally this may reveal a certain degree of vanity, but psychologically it is a healthy point. It is known that when they are sick, whether mentally or physically, people lose any desire to appear at their best.

THE EVOLUTION OF FASHION

Fashion evolves, either speedily or slowly, but it never occurs with an explosion. There is development in stages, even in times of rapid communication, and the sole concession to make on this matter is that most aware designers will project a radical change simultaneously, although in different hemispheres and countries.

For instance the New Look, although apparently explosive in timing, had its beginnings just before the 1939 war. In that year it was possible to see indicative points to what became the New Look. The war of course stopped the progression of this look, and it was only when in 1947 conditions made it possible in terms of cloth production and manufacture, that the full impact was launched in Christian Dior's collection. The very short skirt or dress called the mini happened in a parallel manner. An introduction by, incidentally, the same fashion house in 1960 was a failure. No-one would take to the shorter hemline. But some time later this fashion, together with corresponding changes in shape and detail, began on its journey towards total exposure of thighs in normal wear. Over the period of approximately five years until 1970 the skirt level became shorter and shorter and then stayed.

Midi-length clothes were first seen in 1967, but certainly did not catch on until Yves St Laurent and Valentino of Rome displayed them fully in 1970.

THE NEED FOR CHANGE

Change occurs when banality or boredom sets in. It happens throughout the creative world that at one time one particular product of the innovators will be very much sought after. The methods and ideas admired are emulated and bastardized, decadence and a meaningless approach follow and the original idea becomes commonplace. When this happens the time is ripe for change. Intuition allows the creators to anticipate this and start the change to prevent total boredom.

Changes in clothes fashions during the sixties were faster than ever before because for the first time fashionable changes emanated from youth groups and since the young are on the whole volatile and easily bored with one excitement, the need is for the next, and quickly.

Students, especially at art colleges, tend always to have an extra-sensory perception about changes both in clothes and habits, perhaps because they are so involved with perceptions of all kinds. It was the strong visible approval of the wearing of mini skirts from this element of the British population which made it a universal fashion, although it hardly reached the extremes in other countries that it did in England. It is another example of fashion becoming less the prerogative of the wealthy and privileged, more a statement from a vast 'in' group of youth. Similarly the appreciation of maxi-length clothes as a total reaction to the previous shortness showed a desire in the extreme to change the order of things in general – another revolution. It possibly showed a reaction against the current strong emphasis on mass production, on mass media, on mass anything, and a desire for all that full-length female clothing would suggest in the social context.

This length of clothing is a direct opposite to functionalism in dress for the present day – but it does reflect a need for change in all social matters. It is a curious remembrance of things past.

Chapter 5 STYLE AND STYLES

It is necessary for the professional designer to be able to (a) recognize and define what constitutes 'style' and (b) identify 'styles'. The phrase 'handwriting' is often used with regard to fashion commodities, but usually denotes the personal mannerisms of a particular designer.

To try to evaluate style, imagine that two women buy the same outfit from a designer. One will understand its implications and wear it with style. The other will wear it and convey no quality at all. Or one woman buys a classic knitted dress from Marks and Spencer or Sears Roebuck and endows it with a quality of stylishness, whilst on the other it simply remains a classic knit dress from Marks and Spencer (or Sears Roebuck). Stylishness comes from the presence of the wearer and may be identified with assurance and sophistication. Being stylish should not be confused with the cult of self-expression, which too easily can degenerate into a sartorial free-for-all.

Possessing this elusive style is the prerogative of persons of highly developed taste – those who understand the rules so well that they break them knowingly but with discrimination.

CLASSIC AND ROMANTIC

Broadly there are two main styles, classic and romantic.

Classic is that which is perfectionist, of established excellence, balanced, reasoned and cool, working to a set of rules, almost anonymous, lacking in obvious emotion; even, idealist, ordered, giving away no clue to individuality.

Romantic is expressionist, exotic, esoteric, emotional in technique, stating individuality, eccentric, even absurd.

These are extreme examples and an imaginary line connecting the two would measure all the grades in between – mainly classic, with overtones of romanticism, or romantic detail within a classic framework. For example: a bottle painted in the classic manner is a formal statement, painted according to established precedent, of a bottle, whereas romantically painted it is a bottle which makes one ponder on whether this bottle contains acid or wine. Therefore romanticism adds emotional overtones as opposed to making a factual statement. One can draw a parallel in fashion. A classically dressed woman will give nothing away

A pre-1914 classic Burberry. *Courtesy Burberrys*

Virtually unchanged for fifty years, a Burberry of the mid-1960s. *Courtesy Burberrys*

about her character, whereas if she were romantically dressed, many facets about her could be discovered from all the very personal items she was wearing. One point about this is that it is possible that the face and attitudes of the classically dressed woman will take on more importance as the eye of the beholder will, clothes-wise, solely be aware of harmonious and perfectly proportioned areas and look to the living woman for the alleviation of this cold perfection. Alternatively, romantically designed outfits may take all interest away from the person herself. Both examples could show varieties of the 'clothes horse'. Narrow the whole argument further and one could say that classic is formal and intrinsically severe, while the romantic offers involvement, allusion.
Classic clothing has come to be understood as very simple, unextreme, at worst dreary. By romantic one usually means pretty and feminine. The 'classic tailormade', 'classic twin-set and skirt', 'classic shirtwaist', the 'classic Burberry', these are garments which can go on for decades, basically identical, with only the slightest deviation to fashionable trends. On the other hand, consider what was once termed the classic court shoe! This meant a completely untrimmed or decorated shoe with a heel of anything from one and a half to four inches in height. But study the various differences in shape through the years. It is remarkable how a small article, supposedly termed classic, can change into such a variety of shapes.
It is sometimes difficult to see how modern, contemporary or futuristic design can be classified as romantic or classic. If, however, the intentions are analysed, the distinction will become quite clear. For example, the jumpsuit, inspired by the industrial boiler-suit, and the obsession with functionalism in a technological age, gives an illusion of speed, efficiency and functionalism. This slick, pared-down boiler suit is in fact a pretence and so a romantic conception.
A parallel may be drawn by considering the pastoral peasant clothes affected by Marie Antoinette and the court at Versailles. This, of course, reached the far end of pretence and entered into realms of fantasy.
The confections designed by Paco Rabanne utilizing inflexible metal or solid plastic linked together on chainmail principles are new in so far

as they are light-weight and use apparently indestructible stuffs to achieve glamour. When first invented, linked metal was very weighty and was of course intended for protection. The only use considered appropriate for it in women's wear until the mid-sixties was for jewelry or purses.

Most clothes considered specifically modern have in fact romantic overtones in style. It is the materials and details newly developed, plus methods of manufacture into garments, which can be termed modern. For instance, welded seams (as opposed to conventional stitching); the use of zip fasteners; moulded body shapes instead of shapes being cut and sewn; burr fastening; plastic materials; bonded fibre cloths which are disposable; these are new and modern. They have never been known or produced previously in history, and are of this age.

The designed goods however have hardly changed; it is method and material which make for modernity in clothing.

THE PLACE OF VULGARITY

The definition of vulgar is common or commonplace, but the word generally signifies crudity, excess, brashness, and lack of polish. Try to imagine 'beautiful' vulgarity. In fashion articles, this term may be applied to designs that are witty. A general level of taste must be achieved before full appreciation of the term vulgar may be exercised. Certain contemporary clothes for stage and screen can show this quality. Excess or over-statement qualifies for the label of vulgarity; for instance, a Pearly Queen outfit, beautifully made, is a splendid example of beautifully vulgar. The vulgarity is in the over-statement of the design and decoration. Completely fringed formal dresses show vulgarity through over-statement of movement. The whole delicate problem of making use of conscious vulgarity rests on a knife edge. Too little and there is no point, too much and you come a cropper!

Chapter 6   HAUTE COUTURE; BOUTIQUE;
          READY-TO-WEAR.

The top level of clothes and fashion making has in the past been called the haute couture. This means made-to-measure clothes, virtually made by hand, fitted to perfection to each particular client. The original design of such made-to-measure clothes has to be translated to enhance or disguise various features of the client. The high prices commanded are the result of the service, workmanship, originality of design, and the fine materials that are used. These would include luxurious silks, wools, cottons and fur skins. The client pays for the initial ideas and also for every factor of the clothes production scheme, including superb craftsmanship and a publicized name.

HAUTE COUTURE: THE SYSTEM
In the classic couture, the general system has been as follows: the design studios; the workrooms, designated as tailoring, evening dress or daywear; the fitting rooms; the showrooms and the models' *cabine*. After the designer has selected the fabrics for his new collection, from representatives of all the good textile firms or trimming firms, he starts on his designs. In the case of famous couture houses, the cloth, the design and the colour may be reserved for that one house and therefore be exclusive to it. The various workroom managers join in the discussion about points of design, and a toile – a garment made in rough calico – is made up to a certain model's measurements. It may even be made on her. This is modelled before the designer or may be seen on a dummy or dress stand. The toile may be discussed by the designer and the *vendeuses*, the saleswomen. From that point the design is made up, finished and given all the accessories ready for the first showing. The number of fittings and amount of effort to achieve the right effect are considerable. One seamstress or tailor will work on the garment from start to finish. A tailoring hand will never work on the lightweight clothes, or vice versa. The cutting and the finishing is done in that one workroom, and the manageress is responsible for everything produced in that room.

The *vendeuses* are the women responsible for customers and their orders, and indeed for their fittings, although they will ask fitters to do the work that belongs to each workroom. It is the *vendeuses* who persuade or dissuade clients from choosing the same clothes as another member of their 'set' may have ordered. It is the *vendeuse* who gets commission on her clients' clothes. Throughout, the rule is personal service. Even the manufacturer who buys clothes for copying has a *vendeuse* who looks after him and is responsible for dispatching his orders.

We are discussing exclusive clothes, constructed with enormous thought and attention, and so the flavour throughout the couture house is one of personal effort and care.

THE BOUTIQUE

Schiaparelli was the first to include a boutique in the main dress house, filled with accessories and small slightly cheaper items for the well-dressed woman's wardrobe. Usually boutiques were filled with rather 'gay novelties' (a ghastly phrase – but you know what I mean). They never impinged on the main collection of grand clothing. After the second world war, the French *Maisons de Couture* recovered as a result of the great influence of American buyers, who were buying not only privately but also for department stores or production firms. Almost every design house opened its own boutique, enabling them to sell make-up, perfumes, lingerie, sweaters, little dresses, etc. This phase was epitomized by the house of Dior. In the thirties it was Chanel who proved that a million could be made with a signature perfume, and in the fifties it was Dior who increased sales into every facet of women's wear. But nevertheless it was also possible to order clothes from the Dior boutique and still have one fitting. This was an innovation. They *were* Dior clothes – but not of such intricate styling as those in the main collection and sold less expensively. The Dior empire spread into gloves and undergarments, scarves, jewelry, bags, stockings, children's wear (Baby Dior), and even items for men. Recently in America it has ventured into the field of complete men's wear – like Lanvin and Cardin, and latterly St Laurent.

Boutiques now have become really big business, when organized into a chain of shops belonging to one firm. In this instance the goods are bought in from any manufacturer, and as such it is a debasement of the word. Over the past five years anyone opening a shop dealing with women's wear has called it a 'boutique'. The closest approximation to the original boutique is the small young manufacturing boutique selling original clothes not available on the mass market. On the other hand, the big French couture designers – in particular St Laurent – have themselves opened up wherever possible. St Laurent virtually has an empire throughout western Europe and the States, in his boutiques called 'Rive Gauche'. Obviously to supply such a number of shops, these currently fashionable Yves St Laurent clothes must be mass-produced, though in rather a superior manner and most certainly with a better finish than the normal medium-priced mass production garment. The prices charged for the designer's clothes are *not* modest, and one pays for the exclusive name. This exclusiveness lies in the *name* as opposed to the exclusive *design* made for a minute handful of wealthy clients.

READY-TO-WEAR

Ready-to-wear means just that – one can purchase immediately and in fact be able to walk out of the shop in the garment. This term embraces the whole gamut of price levels and always means mass production work, usually of high quality and probably with some handwork entailed. During the late forties and fifties almost every good-class ready-to-wear firm bought from Paris toiles, garments or patterns, and excellent copies of the original were made at a far smaller cost. Frequently a somewhat complicated original design would be purchased, simply because several items or ideas could be culled from the single source. This design may have been produced as a faithful copy. Or alternatively any item of the original design may have been utilized in different permutations, therefore giving more design potential. The latter garments of course would never be sold as faithful copies carrying the couture designer's name.

While ready-to-wear can be very expensive, by use of expensive cloth, time-consuming construction and intricacy of decoration, true mass production denies the use of at least the last two factors. The term has become synonymous with cheapness, nastiness and slipshod finish. This is hardly fair or true, as many good garments are produced by machine methods. Much still depends on the operatives' handling of the very clever machines now available. All handwork must be eliminated, cheaper fabrics must be used and vast quantities of the clothes sold. It is bulk production made to sell quickly and cheaply, possibly causing an unacceptable amount of uniformity.

Using mass production methods, time is the critical factor rather than the price of the cloth. Therefore all the care and precision employed on *every* process of making garments in the haute couture is now concentrated on the production pattern. If this is foolproof and utterly correct in measurement, then the operatives can simply and automatically put the pieces together with little or no thought. The more a machinist stitches up, the more money she will earn, as most are on what is termed piece-work. The system is that each worker is responsible for one operation, e.g. stitching up collars. In modern factories a transporter or moving belt may be used to carry these components to the next stage of operation. The very last operations will be finishing and pressing, depending on the style of the garment. Often work is received on one level of the transporter and the completed item is hung up on a higher level return belt which carries it to the pressing unit or to a checker.

The start in life of a production garment will be similar to that of couture clothing – the drawing from the designer, possibly even making a toile, which is broken down to a flat paper pattern, with all seam allowances marked and notched. The sample machinist, in the design room or near to it, then machines the cut-out fabric together and passes the article to a finisher, thence to a presser. Perhaps a few more examples may be made, to gauge the time taken and to have sufficient samples ready for salesmen. These are the sales samples from which orders are taken. The first sample pattern is corrected after a rough costing has been made, and then the arguments and discussions between designer and production manager begin. The bulk pieces of cloth will have been ordered and delivered, but perhaps some detail in manufacture is costing too much in time. It therefore must be eliminated or adjusted to another, cheaper, quicker way. Very often outworkers or outworking factories are used, whose managers will give a price for producing a specific number of garments, after having made a sample. Use of these factories cuts the overhead cost of the initial firm, which then is not forced to maintain a large work force at slack times.

The outworker may be knocked down on price, but once agreement is reached the bulk cloth will be dispatched to his factory, plus patterns, linings and trimmings, and his job is to return the completed and agreed number of garments. If he is clever he can by squeezing here and there save on fabric, by making a more economical 'lay' of paper pattern on to cloth. This extra cloth is called 'cabbage' and is considered his perks, for him to sell off or make up into clothes ready to sell. The term rag-trade is really a description of the fantastically frenetic mass production end of the fashion trade. It is extremely tough because the competition is enormous and the pressures are acute.

For many years the mass production firms have shown seasonal collections as is the practice of the couture businesses. There now appears to be a change in policy, and gradually, as a direct result of competition from small boutiques, there is a tendency to produce fewer samples but much more frequently than twice a year.

This of course creates new problems in cloth buying and production. But it does mean that very fast changing whims or fads in fashion can be coped with by larger manufacturing companies who would otherwise lose a profitable source of income to the firms specializing in smaller numbers of quickly produced fashions.

The advent of complicated machinery, because of labour costs getting higher and higher all over the world, should mean that mass production will get better and better, possibly at the cost of individuality in methods and design. But each action causes a reaction and perhaps the cult of individuality during the latter part of the sixties is the unconscious reaction against what would seem inevitable total mass production and anonymity in clothing.

Chapter 7 THE PROFESSION

So far the rag trade, the haute couture, the ready-to-wear, the boutiques, have been discussed, but just how does a graduate fashion designer gain entry into any one of these branches of the trade in a creative capacity?
Assuming a graduate is competent in both design and workshop practice, the most obvious avenues open for exploration are as listed below.

1. Assistant designer or designer
2. Setting up one's own business
3. Freelance designing
4. Teaching
5. Fashion consultancy

While there remain firms who specialize and only produce one type of clothing, for instance coats and suits, there has been a tremendous crossing of fashion territory. Thus furriers will now produce garments in leather, or dress manufacturers will show soft coats and tunic dresses and trousers. A coat firm will produce garments to complement the various coats. At one time, not so long ago, this would have been unthinkable because of the structure of the buyers' profession. By this I mean that only shirt buyers could buy the leather shirt or tunic shown under a particular coat in a collection, and the purchase of a jersey jacket designed as an accessory to a jersey dress was the prerogative of the separates buyer. Great enmities were fostered by this ridiculous system. Once again the influence of the young customer has helped to break this rigid system and therefore to give more freedom of expression to a designer. She has shown preference for outfits which form a coherent look by means of several items planned to be worn together in layers. And therefore store buyers are willing, and manufacturers are able, to spread themselves into other realms.
Although defined categories still exist, such as coats and suits (termed as outerwear), or dresses, the former can stretch into co-ordinates, rainwear or even leatherwear, or indeed evening wear, the latter into evening wear and casual wear. And it should be borne in mind that these directions may only follow a certain logic in design, and any jobseeker will be astute enough to take as examples of his talent designs

which are related to a particular firm's production.

The most important objective for any graduate is to gain experience of the trade in one form or another. These days to go into teaching with no trade experience is foolishness, as one would merely be teaching what one had formerly learned at college; there would be nothing new to pass on. Similarly, fashion consultancy cannot be undertaken professionally without considerable knowledge of the fashion business. This is a job which needs authority and persuasion.

Working as a freelance designer one needs contacts, and a great talent for discipline, reliability and organization.

These are jobs which would perhaps put too much strain upon a student fresh from college, with little authority as yet.

WORKING AS AN ASSISTANT DESIGNER

Unfortunately this term is often used as bait by firms to acquire sketchers or beginner pattern-cutters. While these occupations may be *part* of an assistant designer's job, they should never be the whole. Often one may be told that only people with some experience need apply for a certain position, and one way to have acquired a little experience is while still a student to spend the long vacations with a firm of repute.

Although the ambition of many a graduate designer is to start working as *the* designer within a firm, such a position holds much responsibility, the final responsibility of the livelihood of many workers in the company. If the range does not sell, the company loses money and eventually employees lose their livelihood. Sureness, knowledge and decisiveness can rarely be expected of a student fresh from studies. It is therefore wiser gradually to acquire these qualities as an assistant designer or as one of a team of creative people.

For instance, in large firms great sums of money are involved in ordering quantities of cloth. With this in mind, a designer must be convinced that the styles will be successful commercially. Also with large production one can only know by experience exactly what a factory can produce in a given time. Certain details or methods may be totally uneconomic, and it is the ultimate responsibility of the designer to realize that time is literally money.

Obviously each firm will have its own idea of the jobs a designer must tackle, apart from being a fund of fashion ideas. The day passes very swiftly with cloth salesmen to see, or complaints on deliveries to be made; with belt people, button people, pleating people, with whom one has discussions. There may be the factory to visit and discussion of production with the factory manager. Correct linings and interlinings must be selected and ordered. Commencing a new collection means the arduous task of making an initial selection of cloth from hundreds of swatches; and very often this is done at home in relative peace and quiet. It may be that a fabric is needed which is entirely out of any manufacturer's range; it is then the designer's job, if no central cloth buyer exists, to organize the availability of the exclusive print, weave or knit desired.

Pattern makers, sample machinists and finishers must be supplied with enough work *all* the time, not merely at collection or range time. It may be necessary to discuss or even demonstrate to sample hands how to do certain processes of making, which shows the importance of a designer's having acquired practical knowledge during training.

Having communication with press and buyers may also be part of the day's work, or indeed discussing with the salesforce the selection of samples to go into the final range. Often, with all that must be done in a day, designers will have little time actually to design in their offices or areas of work. They will therefore often have to do this at home in their own time.

With all these things to be responsible for, it is obviously much wiser for a new designer to work as an assistant, to get used to the pace and indeed methods of a firm, and also to gain an idea of who to contact for specific jobs to be done, and of course to learn names of fabric firms and accessory firms who specialize in certain commodities. Having an idea of various import duties and taxes on articles and cloth is useful too, as is knowing the cost of time in production. Above all, being able to communicate with the production manager and in fact with all the people who work with one is of paramount importance. Tact is an asset. Once used to all these matters, which are part of being professional, you are then equipped to take *full* responsibility either in the present firm or in

another where you may find a higher paid or a better position.
It is extremely difficult to enter the trade at one level of, say, very inexpensive merchandise and move into a high-priced goods firm afterwards. If a really good name has been made with the former, then the level may be raised, but usually a designer keeps within the same type of production and merchandise cost. He or she tends to get labelled with the particular level of trade in which he or she has worked.
Some firms will allow their designers to work on freelance commissions provided that the market is quite different. Thus, while working mainly in dresses it is possible to do freelance collections for shoe firms or rainwear companies.

FREELANCE PRACTICE

For most young designers it is better to start with a full-time job and then make one's way into freelance work, as the knowledge gained in everyday work will help towards a better understanding of professional habits and methods. It depends very much on the freelance commission. This might be simply for one outfit for receptionists for a firm, or it could be a complete collection (seasonal) for a garment manufacturer. The job might be to design and make one or two garments for advertising purposes, commissioned by an agency, or indeed a pilot range of children's clothes or even dolls' clothes. There is no end to the possibilities.
Those commissions involving seasonal collections entail discussion of finances on a rather more complex scale than a single fee for a single job. Frequently a retainer is offered plus a comprehensive fee per collection. A retainer of so much a year should ensure that the designer does not produce similar collections for competitive firms. It is of course negotiable as to whether a percentage of sales is paid to the designer. Much depends on whether the designer has made a respected name with previous work, and obviously higher fees may be commanded in this event. Payment is rarely prompt, so one must be assured of some other income to live on. No freelance designer worth his or her salt would simply produce a range of drawn designs. One may be given cloth samples or have to provide one's own as part of the service, but in any event it is imperative to watch over the sample-making stages at the firm's

premises. So much can be misinterpreted without the designer's critical eye to correct; and many a collection has been totally unrecognizable to the originator of the designs when these frequent visits have been omitted.

One word of warning. Design work should never be left with a firm unless paid for. It is always possible to return again for another interview. It must be fully understood that there is no patent system to cover clothing designs and therefore no protection whatsoever in the event of ideas being copied, without actually having been purchased. It is a simple matter for an unscrupulous firm to use a photostat machine in another office in the matter of minutes, so even a disappearance of the designs for such a short time could be detrimental to the designer.

Slides or transparencies could of course prevent such methods, but are not very satisfactory, since they are small and details can be missed. A well-designed folder or folio of manageable size containing neat presentations of work is by far the best way to present designs.

STARTING A BUSINESS

Starting a small business is beset with difficulties, but it is not impossible, even for those with little experience and money behind them. The intelligent thing to do, on the first count, is to join a small firm and learn how it is run. To start your own firm, money, determination and ceaseless hard work, the necessary talent, and the ability to plan and organize are all that are needed.

The rise and fall of many small manufacturing boutiques proves their dismal lack of rudimentary knowledge of business methods. Being able to correspond in a business-like manner will set the tone of the way in which a firm is conducted.

Before attempting to find the necessary money from backers, the cost, purpose and production of the proposed enterprise should be determined as follows:

    The cost of premises, including rates, electricity, water, gas, telephone and insurance.

    The cost of staff, including cleaners, a book-keeper, etc., and taking into account their insurance (SET in the UK).

> The cost of machines and equipment, including cutting tables, chairs, shears, weights, pressing units, electric kettle, etc.
>
> The cost of fabrics and haberdashery for first samples and for stock
>
> Fees for lawyer and accountant. There are some who specialize in the fashion trade.
>
> The cost of owning or hiring transport – cars or vans.
>
> The amount of petty cash needed per week.

Work out the cost of borrowing money, and the methods of doing so with the help of a bank manager or accountant.

Budget at least for a year. Minor details such as invoice and sales books, billheads and letter heading, labels for clothes, must also be added to the final costings, as must any graphic designer's fees for their services on design and layout.

Decide on a minimum of staff necessary for efficiency, including one person with a knowledge of book-keeping. There are agencies for practical staff, i.e. machinists, cutters and finishers, and a register of outworking factories is available.

When the basic cost and structure is completed satisfactorily, approach the sources of money. Anyone investing money will expect interest to be paid, such as so much percent on the loan and on profits, and will state periods of time involved for repayment.

If and when these negotiations are settled, the really exciting work of setting up begins. To spend valuable capital on expensive decoration can be wasteful, as is the purchase of unnecessary equipment. Remember that pleating, buttonholing, embroidery, even final pressing can be done outside by other specializing firms.

Ensure that cloth used for sampling is available in the necessary bulk and can be promptly delivered. It is more than likely to be later than the date specified and this will hold up production for hard-won orders. Keep to a minimum collection of clothes, possibly based on a particular basic pattern, as it is uneconomic to use many.

If there is no retail outlet, i.e. a shop belonging to the concern, contact appropriate fashion buyers, and also fashion editors for appointments to show the collection, be it five garments or twenty-five. Publicity and public relations are all part of the designer's job. Publicity can be very valuable, particularly in the national press, but make sure as far as possible that the production of any styles so publicized is geared to cope with possible floods of orders. Personal publicity is a different field, but remember it is very expensive to hire the services of public relations firms. In a young firm it should in fact be part of the designer's job to promote sufficient interest.

In the event of delayed delivery date of clothes to a buyer, notify her as soon as possible, suggesting an alternative time, providing it is not completely out of season. If this is not done, orders from that source may never come again.

Bad debts are a nightmare, and more likely to come from small shops than large stores. Payment is never in advance, only when goods have been delivered and found acceptable in quality. A small manufacturing firm cannot possibly afford any non-payment for goods delivered, as the payments are needed for buying in new stock. For this reason some capital should always be in hand.

Expand very cautiously and never without sound advice. It is even more difficult than initially setting up.

Remember that there is no point in showing garments which are completely out of seasonal demand, so study carefully the accepted periods of time for these seasons. With a personal retail outlet attached to the firm, this risk may be taken, but never with any other retail outlet.

TEACHING

Teaching, or lecturing in fashion design, can either be considered as a back-up to freelance work or as a profession. While the presence of some full-time teachers is necessary on fashion design courses, the extra fillip to students that comes from contact with, and instruction by, young practising designers is most valuable, particularly to art schools some distance from the main centres. It is essential that as a visiting lecturer one should have practised professionally; otherwise there is no progression or new learning. Refresher courses for existing full-time staff are no substitute for an enthusiastic instructor with professional authority fresh from the knowledge and exigencies of a lively trade. While backing design and aesthetic teaching one can warn and instruct on conditions and commerce.

The problems and conditions of the industry can never be assimilated in a school, since the functions of the two are essentially different. The stresses and strains of business are completely absent in design and art schools. In any case in a design school, whose function is to produce designers, it could be fatal to put too much stress on the technical side of factory production. The possibility of dulling the creative talents of students by over-exposure to technical study would be too great and too apparent. Ideas and creativity are what stimulate and sell, not simply the fact of producing clothes as smoothly and economically as possible.

It is the professional designer instructing students who can bridge this gap between schools and industry.

FASHION CONSULTANCY

Consultancies are usually only offered to designers who have made a name for themselves, or who have worked successfully for some years in the fashion trade. These jobs can be very well paid. They are ideal for those who can talk well. They are 'guiding' jobs – and one may be consulted for advice on styles, production, colour, etc. And the types of firms who employ consultants can vary from clothing manufacturers in any field to textile firms, advertising agencies or large multiple shops. Some large fashion stores in fact employ an overall fashion consultant. One of their jobs would be to correlate all the departments within the current fashion idiom.

In the fashion design business the opportunities for careers can change with changing times. What you may be doing when you are twenty-five may be very different from your job ten years later. Youthful flair may be replaced by useful experience. Both are marketable commodities.

EARTH IN MOTION

R. V. FODOR

EARTH IN MOTION

THE CONCEPT OF PLATE TECTONICS

with diagrams by John C. Holden and photographs
William Morrow and Company   New York 1978

Copyright © 1978 by Ronald V. Fodor

All rights reserved. No part of this book may be reproduced or utilized in any form or by any means, electronic or mechanical, including photocopying, recording or by any information storage and retrieval system, without permission in writing from the Publisher. Inquiries should be addressed to William Morrow and Company, Inc., 105 Madison Ave., New York, N. Y. 10016.

Library of Congress Cataloging in Publication Data

Fodor, R. V.
   Earth in motion.

   Summary: Explains the theory of continental drift, presents the supporting evidence, and describes how this knowledge is important in locating valuable resources and developing warning systems for earthquakes and volcanoes.
    1. Plate tectonics—Juvenile literature. [1. Plate tectonics]
I. Holden, John C. II. Title.
QE511.4.F63   551.1'3   77-12568
ISBN 0-688-22135-1
ISBN 0-688-32135-6 lib. bdg.

Printed in the United States of America.
First Edition
1 2 3 4 5 6 7 8 9 10

CONTENTS

1 First Ideas 7
2 Structure of the Earth 19
3 The Model 37
4 Scientific Evidence 59
5 Applications in Daily Life 75
   Index 93

For Klaus Keil

1

FIRST IDEAS

A casual look at a world map or a globe quickly reveals that the Earth has seven continents: North America, South America, Europe, Asia, Africa, Australia, and Antarctica. With closer inspection, you may notice that the eastern coastline of South America and the western coastline of Africa would match neatly, like jigsaw-puzzle pieces, if the Atlantic Ocean were removed and the two continents brought together. After still closer examination, you may observe that the eastern coast, or margin, of the United States would fit snugly against the northwest

The coastlines of some continents fit together neatly like parts of a puzzle.

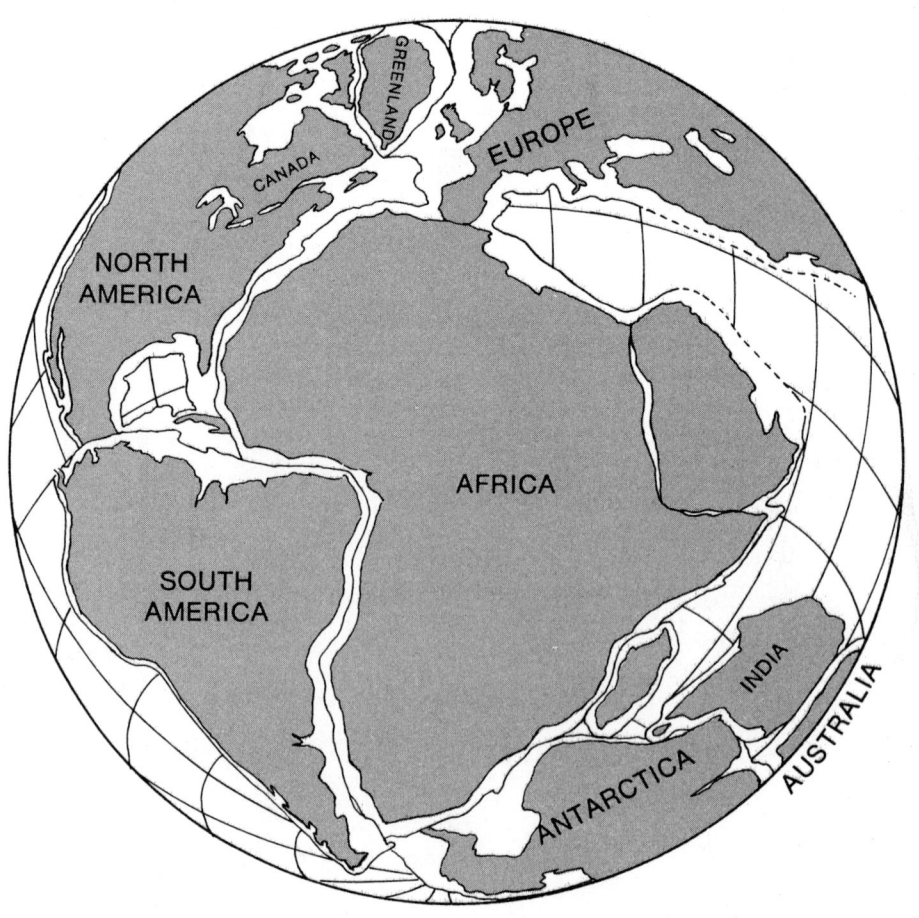

margin of Africa, and that Canada would piece together with Greenland—if the Atlantic Ocean did not separate them.

Could these matching outlines of the continents simply be coincidence, or could they mean that at one time the continents were actually pieced together with no oceans between them? Observations and questions about the outlines of continents and their matching coastlines are not new. As far back as 1620, when some of the world's first maps were drawn, Francis Bacon, an English statesman, drew attention to the outline and the shapes of the continents in his book, *Novum Organum*.

Scientific models, or explanations, to account for the fit among the continents came about several centuries later, however. Around 1900, for example, the Austrian geologist Eduard Suess proposed that at one time in the Earth's history there was a giant continent in the southern half of the world composed of South America, Africa, India, Australia, and Antarctica. He named that landmass Gondwanaland. And, in 1910, the American geologist Robert Taylor suggested that the continents might actually move. He explained mountain ranges as features caused by the continents moving across the globe and buckling up at their margins, much like wrinkled rugs.

Not until 1912, however, did the first real scientific debate begin over the shapes of the continents and whether their shapes meant that the continents were not permanent. It started with the German meteorologist Alfred Wegener. Like scientists before him, he noted the remarkable match of coastlines on opposite sides of the Atlantic Ocean and was impressed by it. Wegener, too, considered that possibly the continents were joined in larger landmasses long ago. But the idea was so preposterous that he soon discarded it.

A few years later, however, Wegener accidentally came across some reports written by paleontologists, the scientists who study fossils. These reports stated that land bridges, or narrow strips of land, once connected South America and Africa. The reason why paleontologists believed land bridges had existed was that the same types of fossils were being found on each continent. They concluded that the animals, when living, must have crossed from one continent to the other and needed bridges to do so.

Recalling his curiosity about the jigsaw-puzzle fits

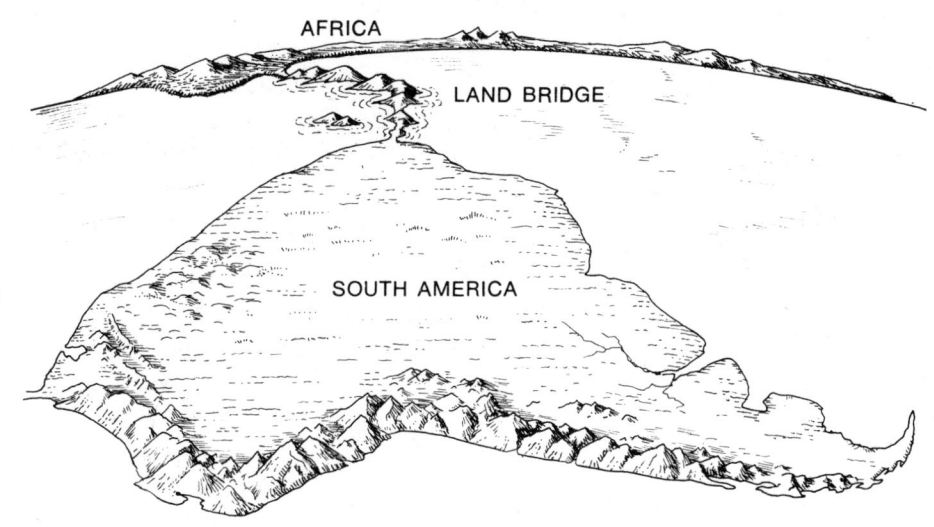

At one time, some scientists believed continents were connected by narrow land bridges.

of the continents, Wegener was inspired to put forth a hypothesis, or scientific idea, on continental drift. He proposed to the scientific community that all the continents were at one time united as a supercontinent—which he named Pangaea—and that during the Mesozoic geologic era (about 200 million years ago) it began to break into individual fragments that drifted across the ocean floors to their present positions. That process, Wegener believed, explained why similar fossils were appearing on different continents and why the continents looked like puzzle pieces.

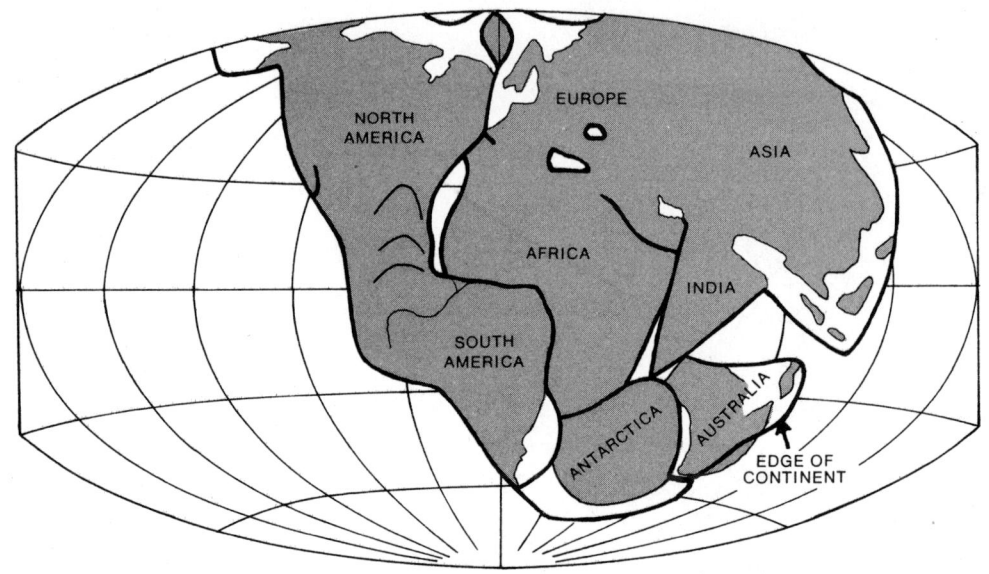

Alfred Wegener was one of the first scientists to state that the continents formed a giant landmass long ago. He called it Pangaea and believed it looked like this.

Wegener viewed the Earth as consisting of continents made of relatively lightweight rock "floating" in the heavier, or denser, rock of the ocean floors. He likened the continents to icebergs in seawater, which may break apart and whose fragments may drift in various directions without sinking. To account for the mechanism that moved the continents, he suggested tidal forces from the sun and moon and pole-fleeing forces that flowed toward the Earth's equator.

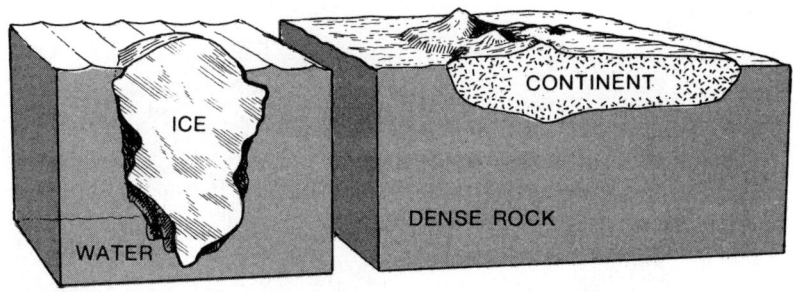

Wegener thought the continents floated apart, like ice in water.

Wegener's concept was indeed fascinating—and controversial, too. From the time he published his book, *Die Entstehung der Kontinents und Ozeane* (*The Origin of the Continents and Oceans*), in 1915, until about 1930, earth scientists argued about continental drift. Alfred Wegener's hypothesis certainly attracted many supporters, but the majority of scientists discredited continental drift, despite the excellent evidence of the coastal outlines and the similar fossil types present on different continents. There was even further geologic evidence of similar rock formations on different continents. Namely, the very distinctive Gondwana Series was observed to be present on South Africa, Madagascar, South America, the Falkland Islands, Australia, and Antarctica—all places which are now separated by water.

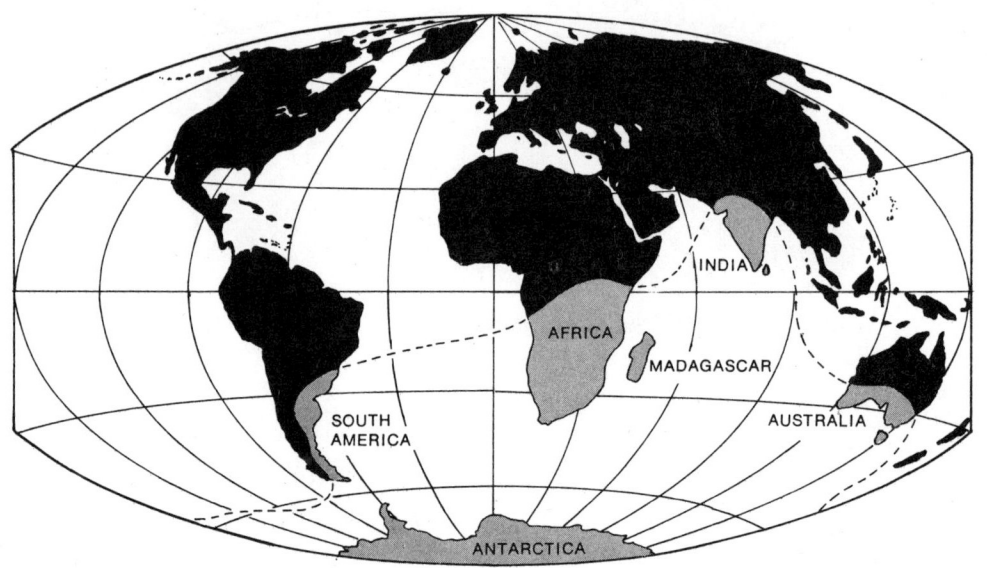

The Gondwana Series of rock formations (gray areas) is present in parts of the world now separated by water, which may mean all this land was connected at one time.

The main reason that the continental-drift hypothesis was disbelieved by most scientists was that Wegener's explanation for the driving forces behind continental drift was weak. It did not seem sufficient to account for the moving of something as permanent and massive as continents. How could a continent plow through the rock of an ocean floor?

Then, in 1928, a well-respected British geologist named Arthur Holmes published an article discussing a force that could possibly drive the continents apart. Holmes proposed the presence of thermal convection currents, or currents of heat, in the interior of the Earth. These currents are much like those that occur in a pot of boiling water, in which hot currents rise to the top, cool, and then sink. Holmes said that as these currents rose up from the interior of the Earth to the base of the continents, they moved outward along the base, stretching and breaking the continental masses apart and dragging them. The explanation was fantastic, and actually more realistic than Holmes was aware of at the time. But there was no scientific evidence that such currents really existed, and Holmes's mechanism for continental drift remained only an interesting idea.

In 1930, Wegener died while on a scientific ex-

Convection currents in the Earth could behave much like those in a pot of boiling water.

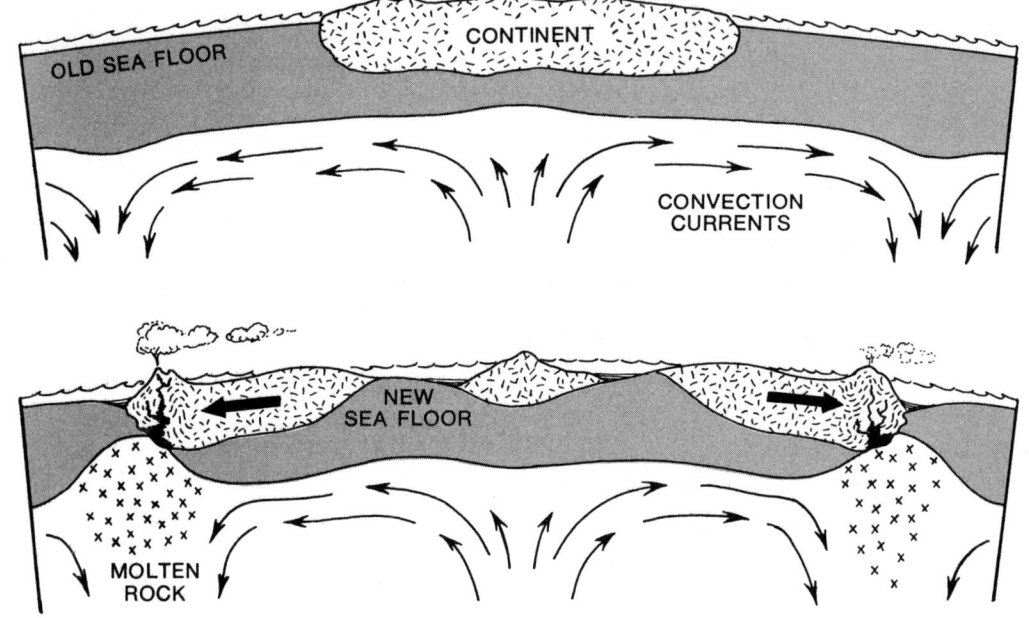

Arthur Holmes thought convection currents in the Earth caused the continents to break apart.

pedition on Greenland. Soon afterward, the concept of continental drift was put to rest too.

Interest in the idea was revived in the 1950's, however. It was inspired mainly by the beginning of detailed exploration of the oceans and by the study of magnetic properties of rocks. By the late 1960's, there was excellent evidence that the continents were indeed joined together at one time, that they did drift apart, and that they were still moving!

Hence, a new field of earth science opened up in the late 1960's, attracting a new group of young scientists. Soon the study of the Earth in terms of moving continents became known as "plate tectonics." Today geologists all over the world continue to study the Earth from ocean basins to mountaintops to provide additional information for strengthening this remarkable concept about the Earth in motion and to unravel its geologic history further.

2

STRUCTURE OF THE EARTH

To understand fully the concept of plate tectonics and the mechanics involved, it is important to become familiar with the structure of our planet. The distance from the surface to the center of the Earth, or its radius, is about 6400 kilometers. Yet no more than a thin skin of about 15 kilometers has ever been seen. Fortunately, there are other ways of obtaining information about these unseen portions of the Earth. Scientists mainly do so by applying some principles of physics and by using highly sophisticated electronic equipment.

The first scientific information about the interior of the Earth became available early in this century. By studying the vibrations, or seismic waves, that

Seismographs record vibrations of the Earth, especially those of quakes.
R. V. Fodor

are produced by earthquakes and travel deep into the Earth, the presence of a core was detected. This core is greatly different in composition from the rocks on the Earth's surface. It is believed to be composed mainly of iron, solid in the center but having a liquid outer portion. The diameter of the Earth's core is about 7000 kilometers, and the top of the core is about 2900 kilometers below the surface of the Earth.

The study of earthquake waves also showed that at a relatively shallow distance from the surface—about 35 kilometers below the continents and about 6 kilometers below the ocean floor—there is material different in composition from both the iron core and the rocks commonly seen on the surface. This region of the Earth is known as the "mantle." It is composed of rock that is rich in the element magnesium, a type that is generally called "peridotite." The mantle extends to the top of the core, a depth of about 2900 kilometers.

At the very outer portion of the Earth, the top 35 kilometers of the continents and the top 6 kilometers of the ocean floor, is what is known as the "crust." Ocean crust consists largely of rock that is

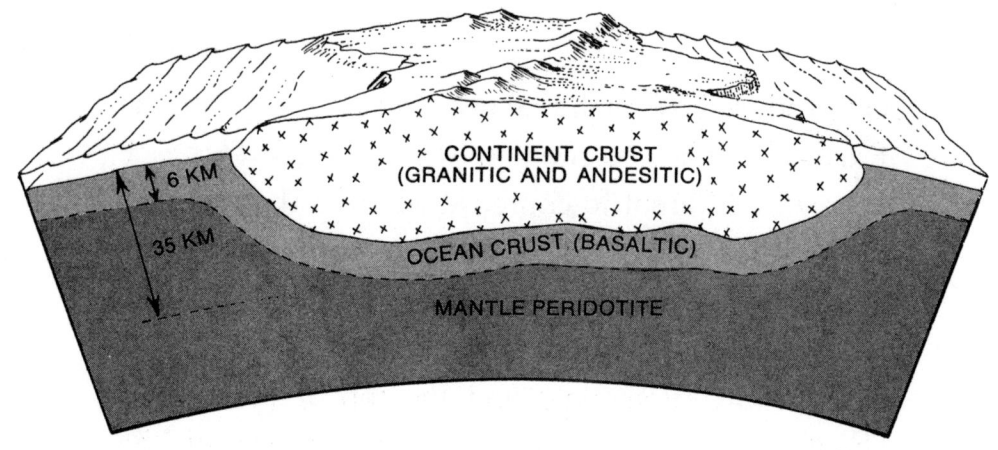

The ocean crust is much thinner than the crust of the continents.

called "basaltic," also rich in magnesium, but in iron, too. In contrast, the crust of continents is composed mainly of material referred to as "andesitic" and "granitic," containing the elements silicon, potassium, and sodium in greater amounts.

The terms *crust* and *mantle* describe the structure of the Earth mainly on the basis of its chemical composition. What is not specified is how solid or rigid these materials are. Therefore, the Earth's structure can be expressed in another way. The very rigid material that includes all of the crust and the upper part of the mantle, to depths of about 100 kilometers from the surface, is called the "lithosphere." Below the lithosphere is mantle material that is believed to be somewhat molten or plastic and is called the "asthenosphere." It extends to a depth of about 300 kilometers. Between the asthenosphere and the outer core is the part of the mantle called the "mesosphere," an area about which little is known.

A look inside the Earth shows
its thin crust, its mantle, and its core.
The crust and mantle can also be thought of
as lithosphere, asthenosphere, and mesosphere.

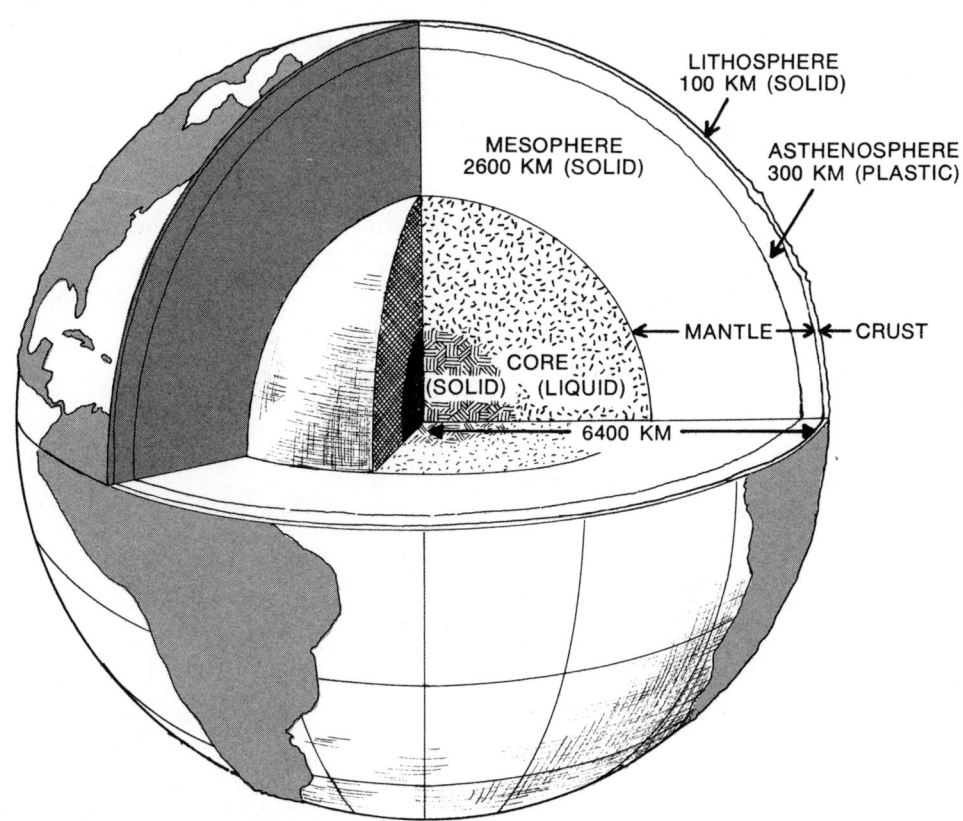

On the surface of the continents, some of the most obvious and familiar features are mountain ranges. What may not be so obvious, however, is that large mountain ranges are restricted to very distinct and often narrow zones. They are not randomly distributed across the landmasses. The Sierra Nevadas in California and the Andes in Peru and Chile, on the western coasts of North and South America, are good examples. Similarly, the occurrences of earthquakes and volcanism on the continents are confined to certain regions. And these earthquakes and volcanic zones coincide with those of the vast mountain

Many continental mountain ranges
are restricted to narrow zones,
as along the western coasts of North and South America.

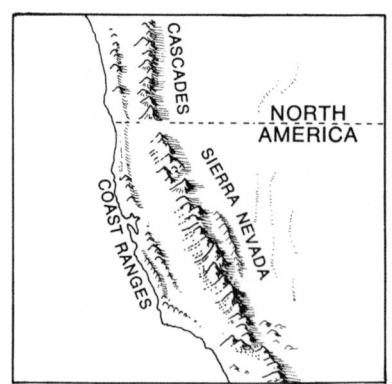
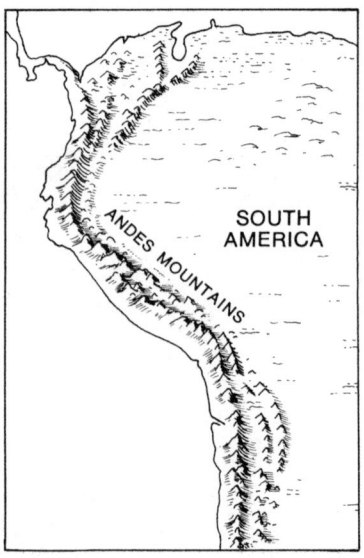

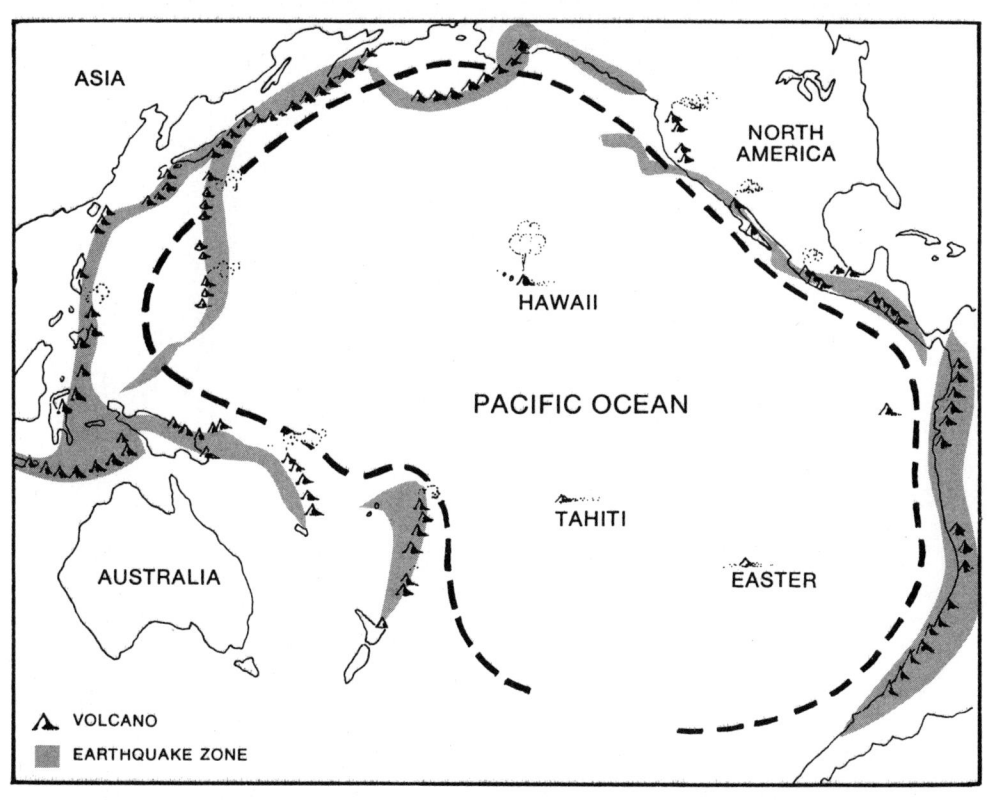

The broken line marks the "ring of fire" that experiences much volcanism and earthquakes.

ranges, as on the western coasts of North and South America. In fact, the entire region surrounding the Pacific Ocean is very active in earthquakes and volcanism and is sometimes described as a "ring of fire."

Scientific research of the ocean basins officially began in 1872 with the three-and-a-half-year voyage

H.M.S. Challenger was the first ship used to study the ocean floors over one hundred years ago.
Reports of the Challenger

of the vessel *H.M.S. Challenger*. From that ship scientists first determined depths of the oceans and sampled material from ocean bottoms. But not until the 1950's was any real progress made in understanding the shape and form of ocean floors. By that

Opposite, top: Small submarines, or submersibles, are used by scientists today to visit and photograph the volcanic rocks of the ocean floor.
Woods Hole Oceanographic Institution
Bottom: volcanic rock on the mid-Atlantic ridge, photographed during a dive in the submersible, *Alvin*
Woods Hole Oceanographic Institution

time, depths could be measured rapidly and accurately by echo-sounding equipment aboard ships and then noted on maps.

The most significant discovery in the oceans was the rugged, volcanic mountain ranges that span the globe in an almost continuous network of 65,000 kilometers. The most prominent and well-studied of the ocean ridges is the mid-Atlantic. It snakes along the middle of the Atlantic Ocean floor from an area farther north than Iceland to almost as far south as Antarctica.

"Midocean ridges," as they are called, even though they are not always exactly in the middle, can be up

underwater mountain chains—midocean ridges

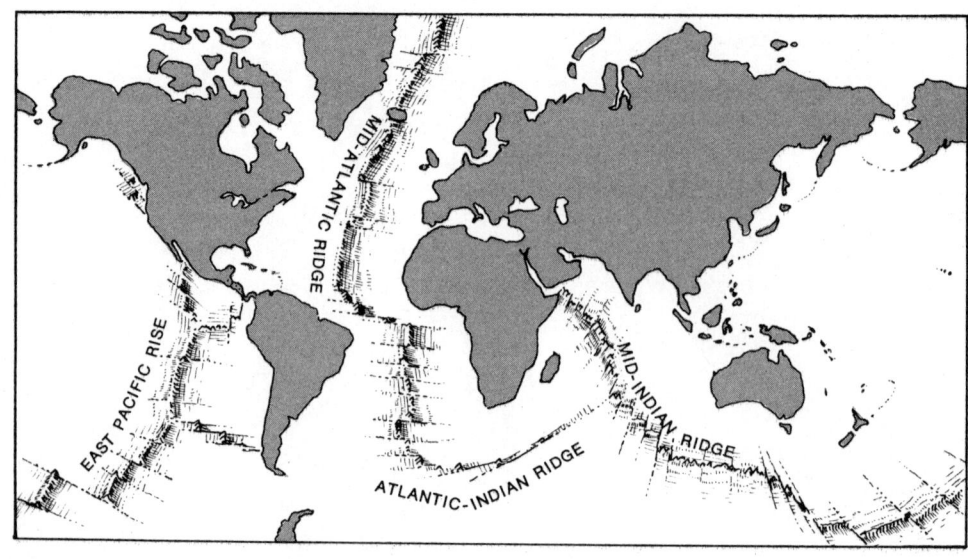

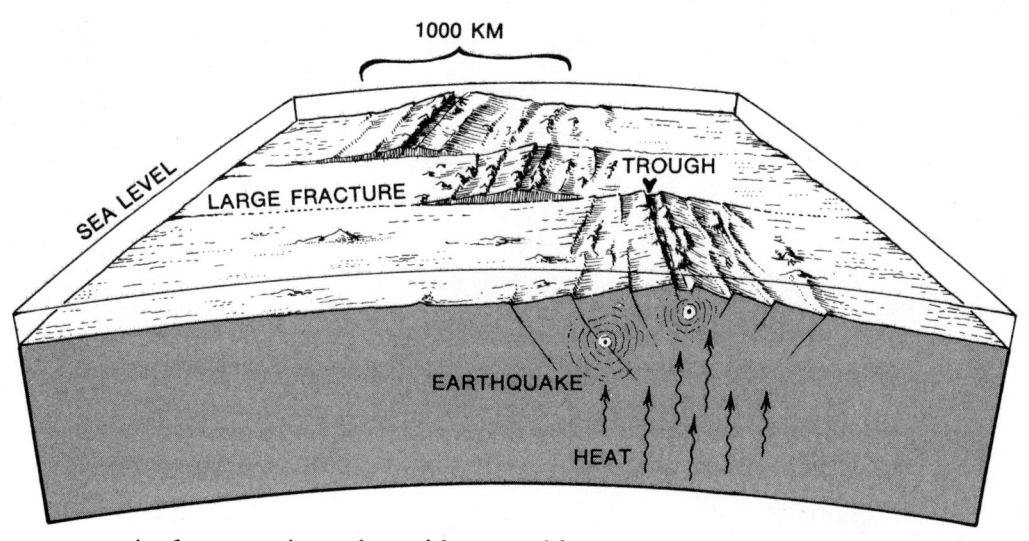

A close-up view of a midocean ridge: these mountain chains are often broken by large fractures.

to 1000 kilometers in breadth and often stand over 4000 meters above the sea floor. A characteristic feature of many is the presence of a trough, or valley, in the crest. These troughs sometimes have floors 12 to 15 kilometers wide and walls that are 600 to 2000 meters high. However, as continuous a girdle as these underwater volcanic mountains form around the globe, they are not without interruption. Every few hundred kilometers, they are displaced and broken into different segments along fractures that were caused by movements in the Earth's crust.

Earthquakes are common to midocean ridges, just

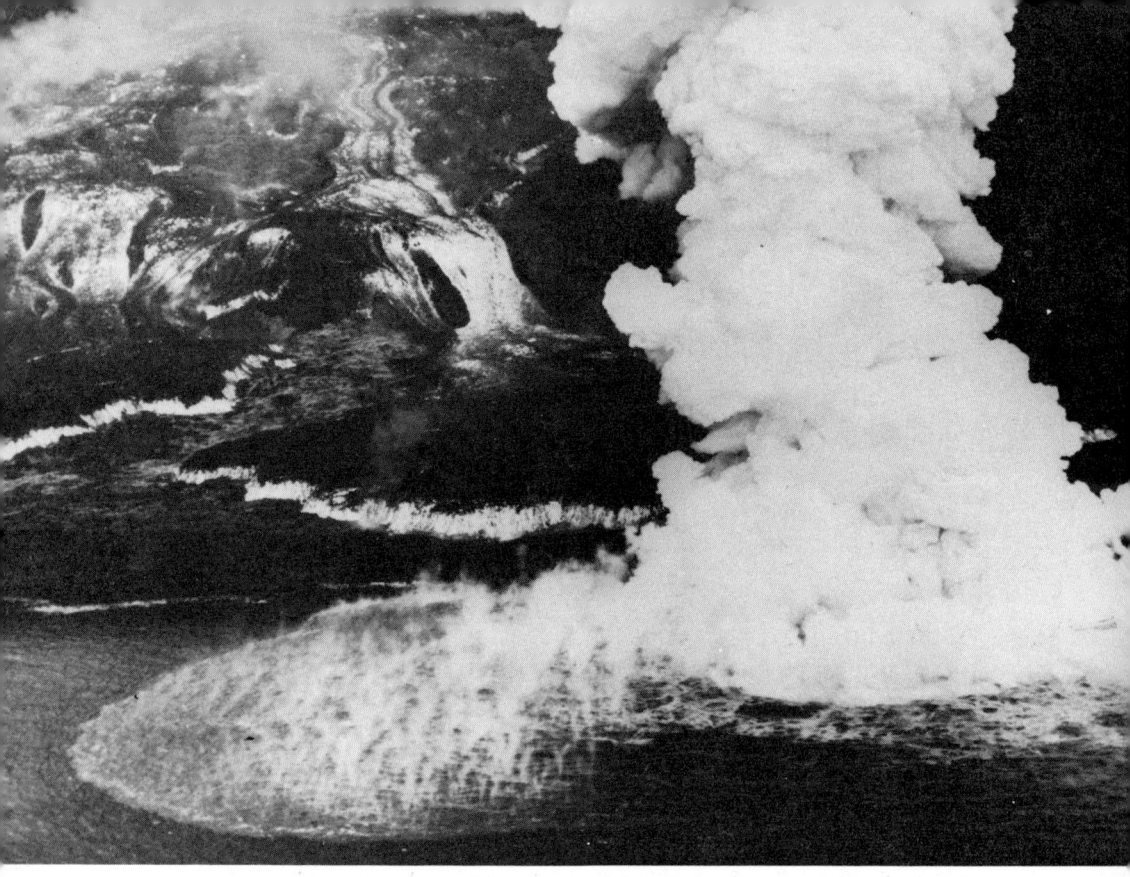

The Hawaiian Islands have been a site of much volcanism for several million years. This picture is of the 1950 eruption of Mauna Loa.
United States Air Force; Hawaii Volcano National Parks

as they are to many of the continental mountain ranges. In addition, a high flow of heat has been measured along the midocean ridges by heat-sensitive instruments. Volcanism along the ridges is related to this heat flow.

Volcanic activity in some areas along midocean ridges was extensive enough to form huge piles of lava that eventually emerged above water. One such region is Iceland. This island shows all the char-

Iceland is made up of volcanoes
that formed directly on the mid-Atlantic ridge;
other volcanic islands lie alongside the ridge.

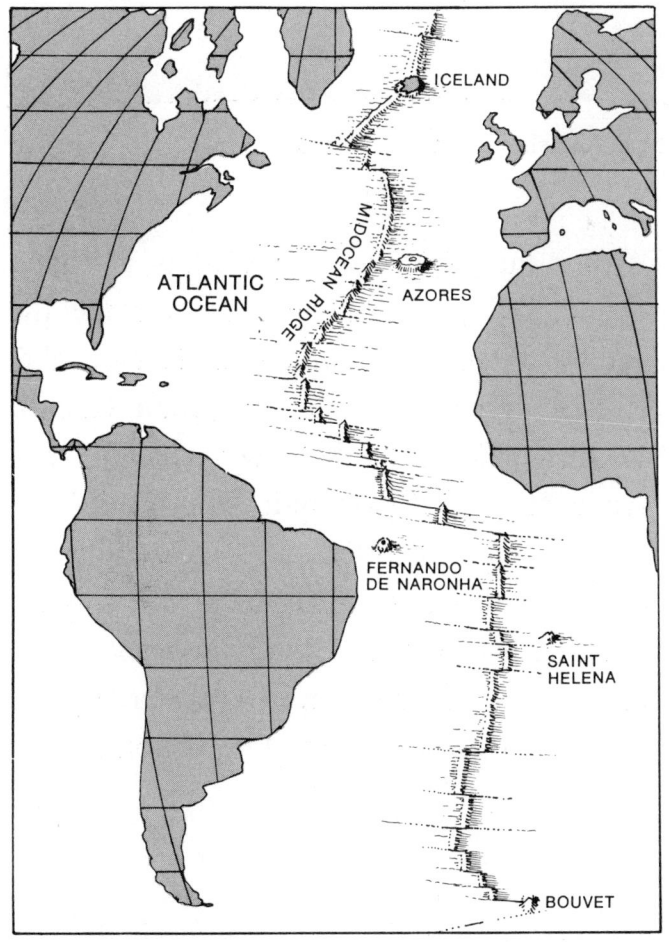

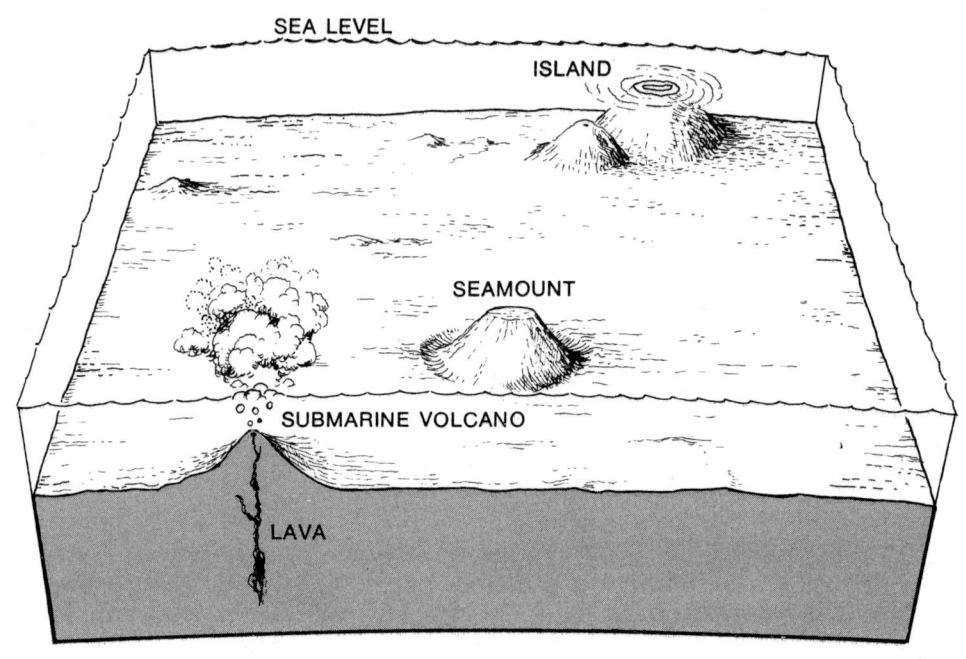

Volcanoes form islands and seamounts.

acteristics of a midocean ridge, including a trough in the middle. Other volcanic islands include the Azores, Saint Helena, and Fernando de Noronha, in the Atlantic Ocean, and the Hawaiian Islands, Tahiti, and Easter Island, in the Pacific Ocean. None of them are located exactly on midocean ridges, however, so Iceland is an exception.

In addition to the volcanic islands like Hawaii, there are hundreds of volcanoes in the oceans where the volcanism may not have been quite enough to build the volcano above water. Or, if some were above water at one time, they since have become submerged. These underwater islands are known as "seamounts."

There are other groups of volcanic islands that are located near continents and are lined up as chains in the form of an arc, or part of a circle. Many of these "island arcs," as they are called, are on the margins of the Pacific Ocean along the ring of fire. One ex-

the island arcs and ocean-floor trenches of the Pacific Ocean region

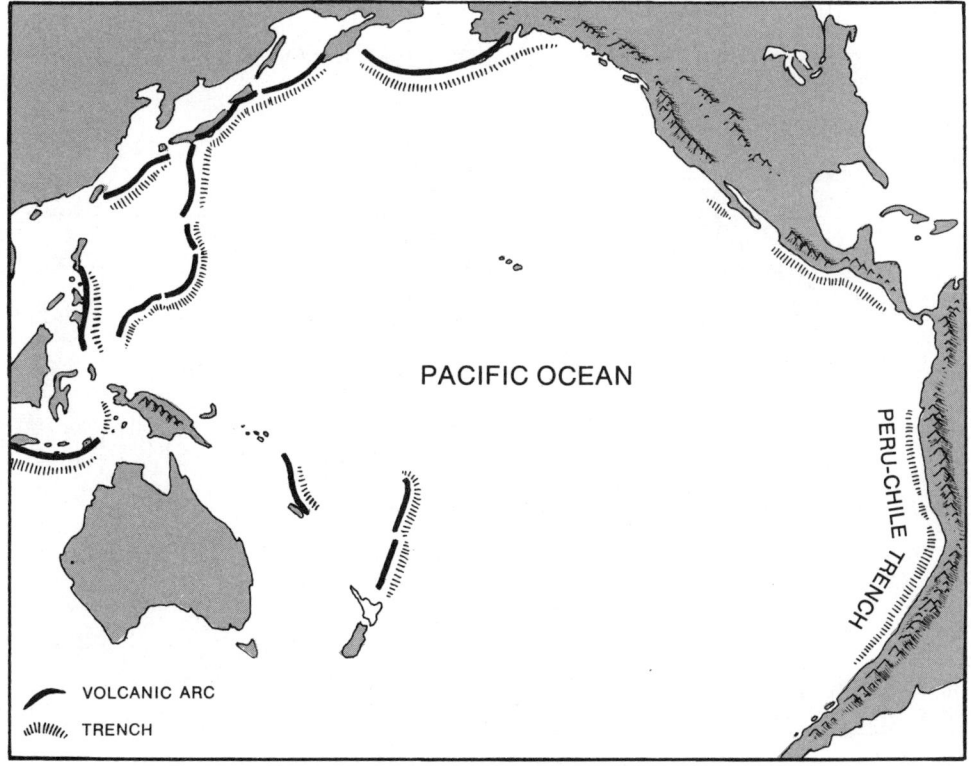

ample is the Aleutian Island arc off the state of Alaska. The West Indies in the Caribbean Sea also forms an island arc. A characteristic feature of island arcs is the high number of earthquakes that they experience.

On the ocean floor about 100 to 200 kilometers away from island arcs, in the direction of the open ocean, are vast trenches. These trenches can be as deep as 11 kilometers, over 3000 kilometers long, and only 5 kilometers wide at their bottoms. There are also trenches present at some continental margins, such as the Peru-Chile trench along the west coast of South America. The distance from the lower

volcanic-island chains in the form of an arc

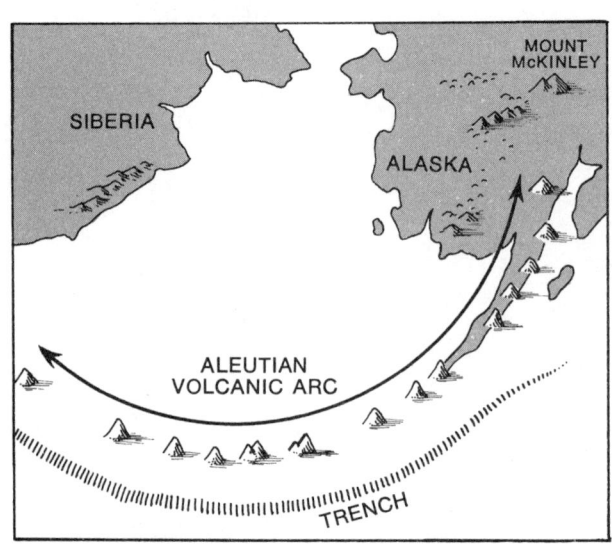
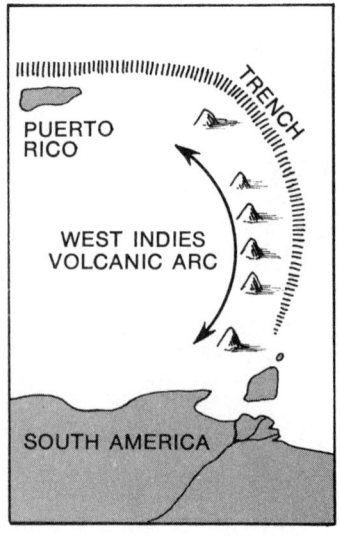

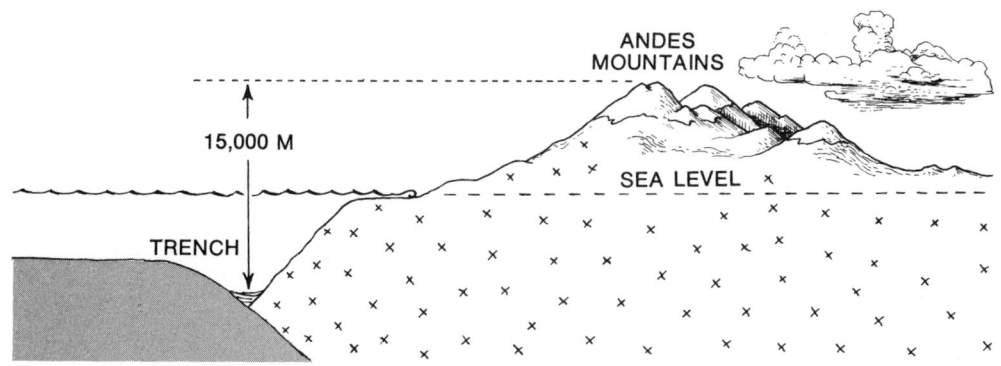

the Peru-Chile trench

part of the Peru-Chile trench to the highest part of the neighboring Andes is about 15,000 meters. In the Pacific Ocean alone, there are about twenty trenches.

The locations of mountain ranges, ocean ridges, island arcs, and earthquake and volcanic activity are all very important in the model that scientists have developed for the concept of plate tectonics.

3

THE MODEL

Although it was not known at the time, the concept of plate tectonics was born in the early 1960's. The two scientists largely responsible for its birth were H. H. Hess of Princeton University and R. S. Dietz of the United States Coast and Geodetic Survey. Each put forth the fascinating idea that the sea

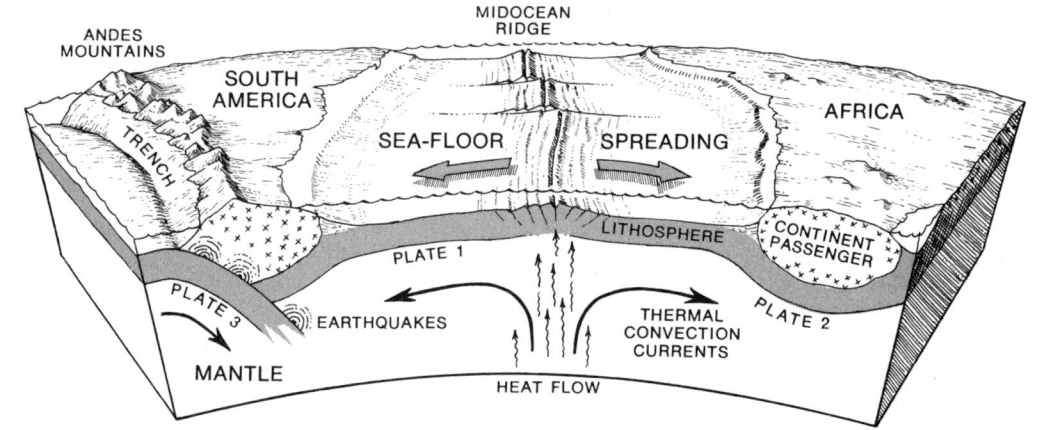

the sea floors spreading away from midocean ridges, carrying overlying continents with them

floors are not permanent, but instead are moving, or spreading, away from the midocean ridges.

The few scientists who still believed in continental drift as presented by Alfred Wegener welcomed this interesting hypothesis as a new approach to the dormant idea. No longer need they think of continents drifting through ocean crust like ships forcing their way through ice. Instead, they could view the continents simply as "passengers" on a spreading ocean crust—a model that many scientists soon found easier to accept than the original idea proposed by Wegener.

The concept of sea-floor spreading pertains to the ocean floors moving in opposite directions away from midocean ridges. The spreading and the volcanism that formed the midocean ridges are thought to be related to heat currents rising from the deep mantle. Although Arthur Holmes in 1928 had suggested the presence of such currents, the theory could not be proven at that time. Since then, evidence that such currents actually do exist in the mantle has become available. For example, the unusually high heat flow measured at ocean ridges has been attributed to thermal convection currents, or currents of heat rising from the mantle.

The sea-floor-spreading hypothesis envisions that these mantle currents rise to the bottom of the lithosphere and spread out. During their horizontal movement in opposite directions away from the ridges, the currents carry the lithosphere along as though on conveyor belts. This process can be compared to hot currents rising in a pot of boiling stew. The currents reach the top, carry the thin scum off to the sides, and then sink.

When the lithosphere moves away from the ridges, new molten rock, called "magma," rises from where it was produced in the mantle to fill the gaps. This upwelling of magma is marked by the majestic mid-

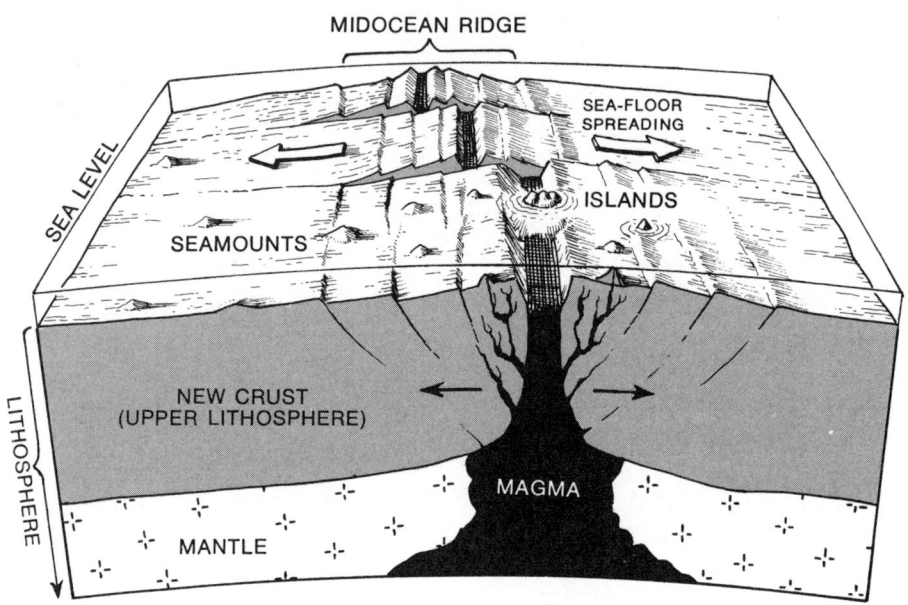

Rising magma cools in the midocean ridges and replaces rock that has spread away.

ocean ridges. Sometimes the volcanism is great enough to construct islands, such as Iceland, along the ridges. According to the sea-floor-spreading model, however, the islands too eventually move along with the spreading lithosphere away from the ridges. Later they may submerge to become seamounts.

Thus, the model for sea-floor spreading proposes that new molten material is continually being added to ocean crust at the ridges. But if large volumes of ocean crust are being formed at ocean ridges, and if

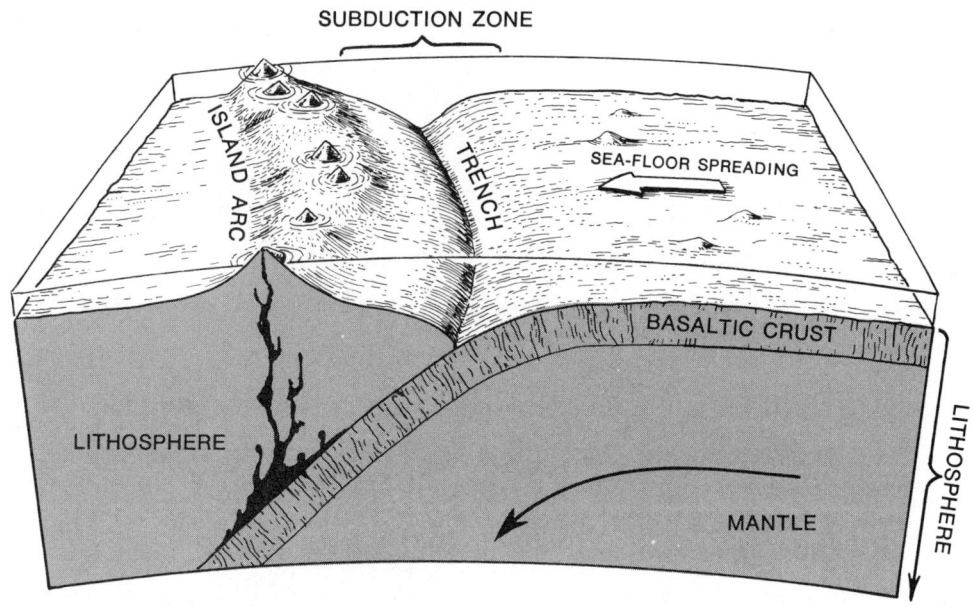

Older lithosphere sinks
into the Earth at subduction zones.

the existing lithosphere is moving away, where is all the material going to? Because the Earth is not growing in size, the older lithosphere must be removed at approximately the same rate that new lithosphere is being added. The sea-floor-spreading idea solves this problem by stating that the old lithosphere bends down and sinks into the mantle. And the areas where the lithosphere dips back into the Earth are at the deep ocean trenches near island arcs and certain continental margins. These zones of sinking lithosphere are called "subduction zones."

Hence, the Earth is recycling itself. It is continually creating new lithosphere at ocean ridges and "swallowing" older lithosphere in subduction zones.

But the Earth is spherical in shape. And on its outer shell there are many midocean ridges from which lithosphere is moving away, and many trenches where it is being subducted. Therefore, in order to move in different directions across a sphere, the lithosphere must break into many individual plates or sections. Thus, the name plate tectonics was devised. It describes more accurately what is happening to the Earth's outer shell than the old name of continental drift. The word *plate* refers to lithosphere

The Earth recycling: lithosphere is created in some areas and destroyed in others.

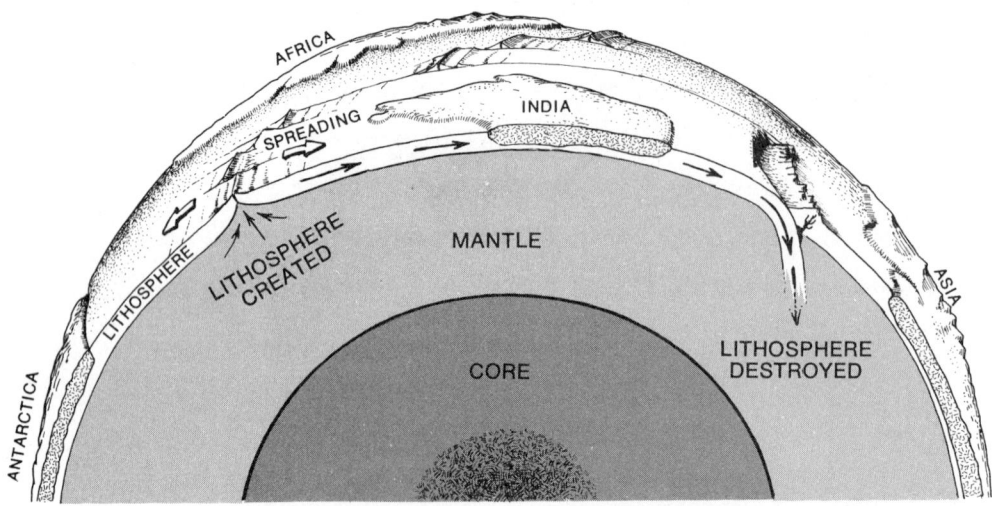

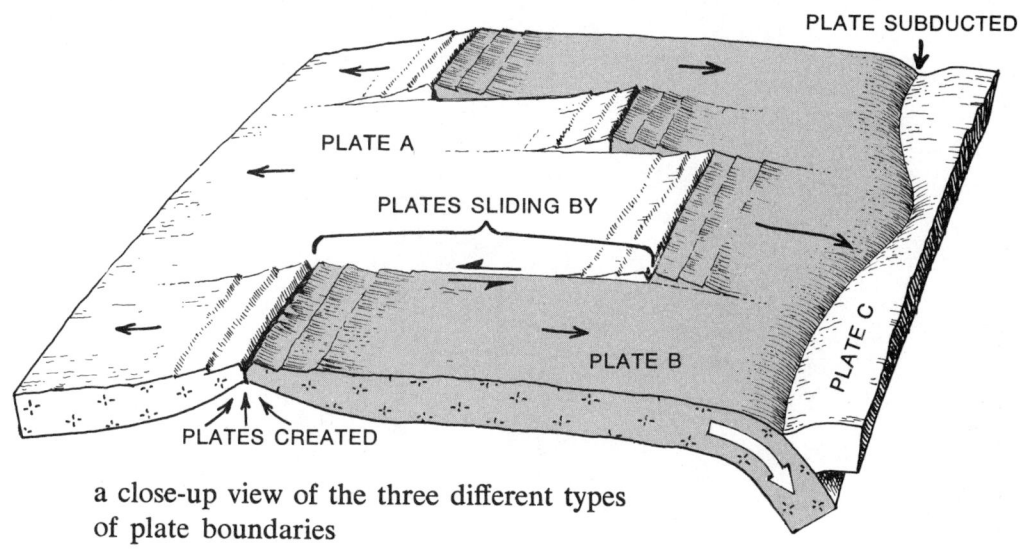

a close-up view of the three different types of plate boundaries

being composed of several segments, and the word *tectonics* refers to movements in the crust.

The concept of plate tectonics, as believed today, states that the lithosphere is composed of six major plates—American, Eurasian, African, Indian, Antarctican, and the Pacific. Each of these plates is broken into many smaller ones. Some of the plates consist partly of continental crust and partly of oceanic crust; others, like the Pacific, are entirely oceanic. Plate margins, or boundaries, are of three types: those at the ocean ridges, where the plates are being created; those at ocean trenches, where plates are being subducted; and those at fractures, where plates are only sliding past one another.

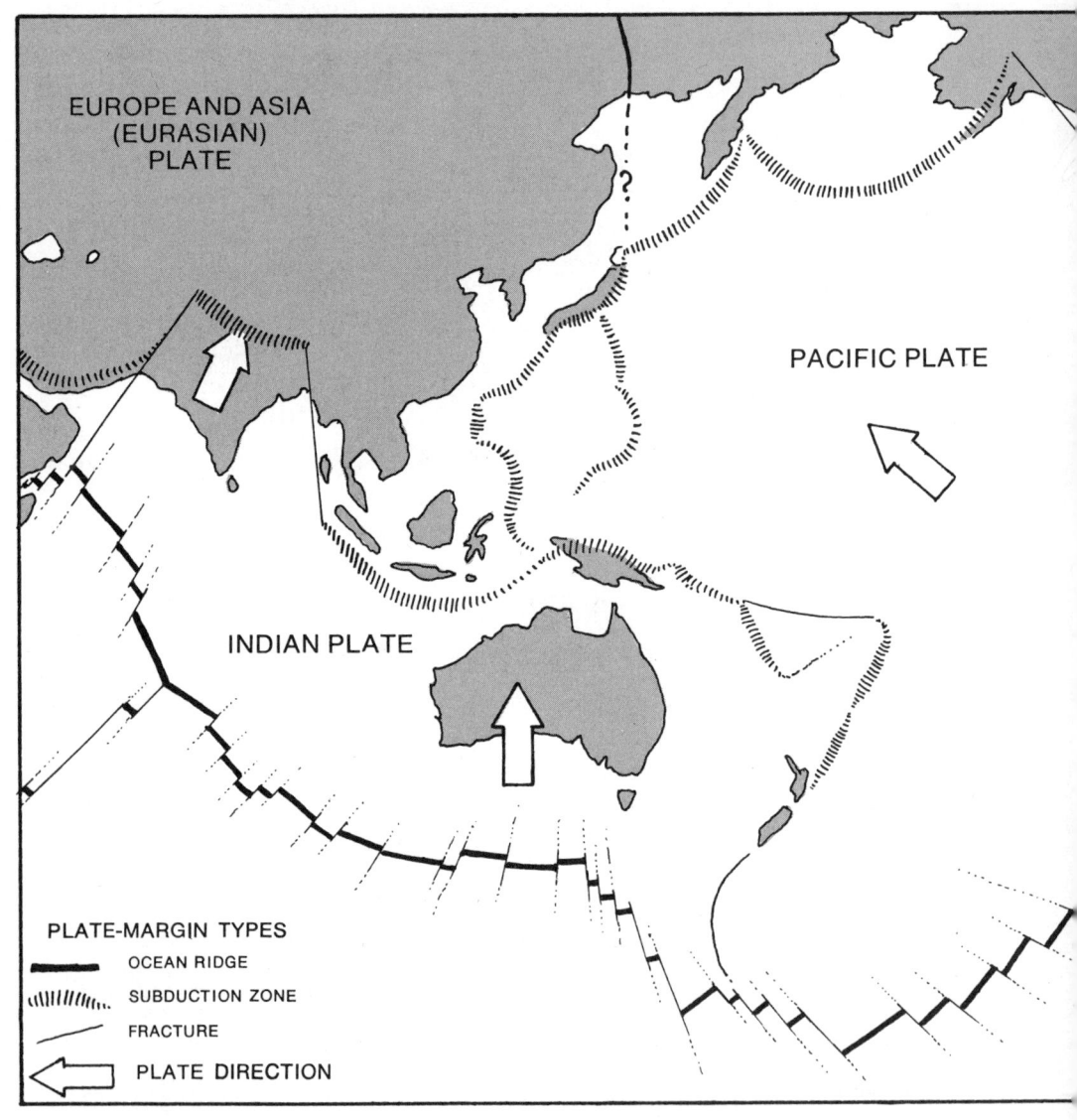

the major plates of the Earth
and the direction in which they are moving

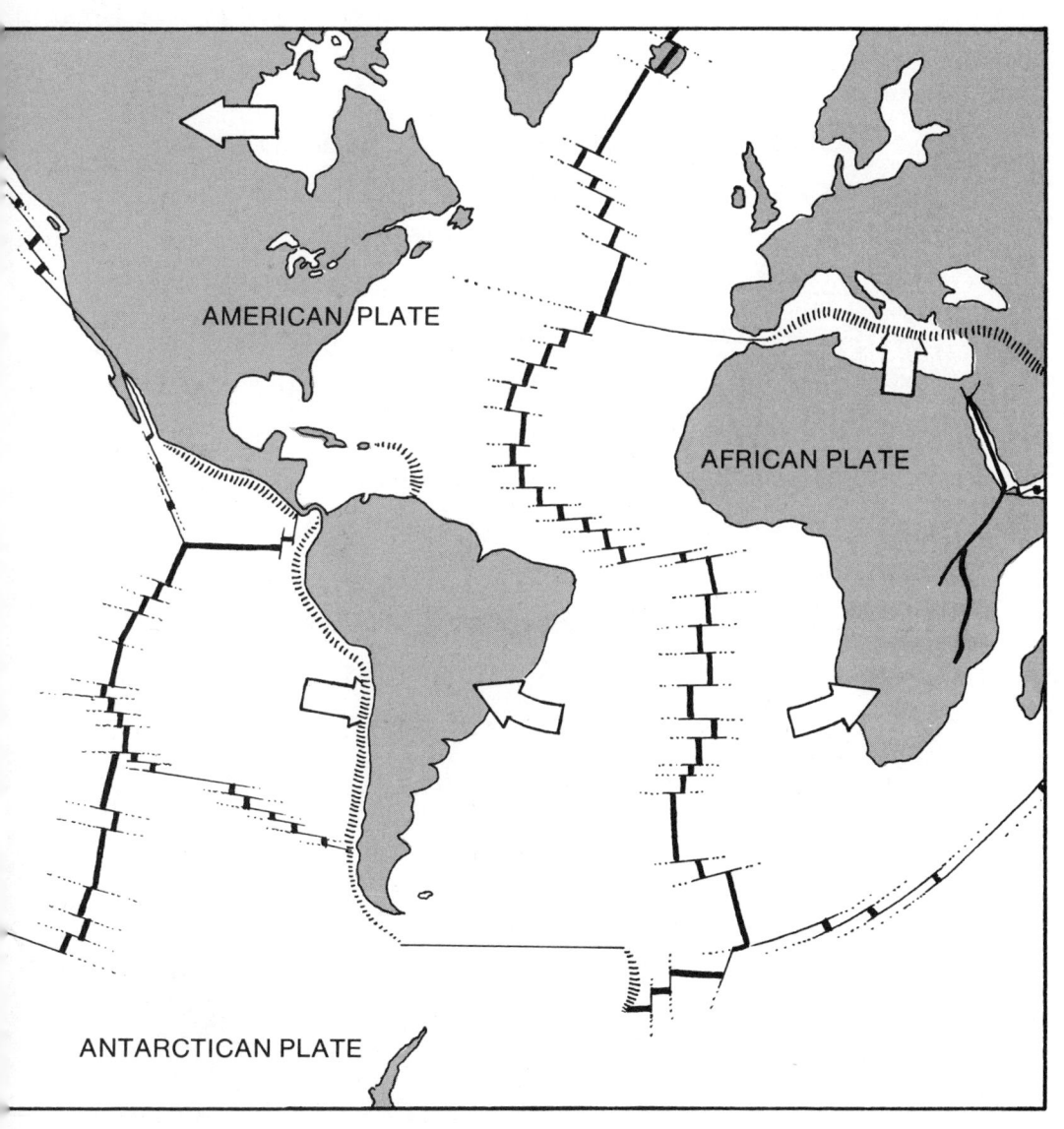

Each of the plate boundaries is marked by earthquakes and volcanic activity, and some by mountain building. All of these geologic events are greatest at the areas of plate subduction. The reason for intense earthquake activity at subduction zones, for example, is that as one plate sinks beneath the leading edge, or front, of another, great pressures are produced as the plates rub against each other. When the pressures between two plates become so great that the Earth's crust breaks, earthquakes result.

The plate-tectonics concept also proposes that the development of the island-arc systems throughout

Earthquakes occur where one plate slides beneath another in a subduction zone.

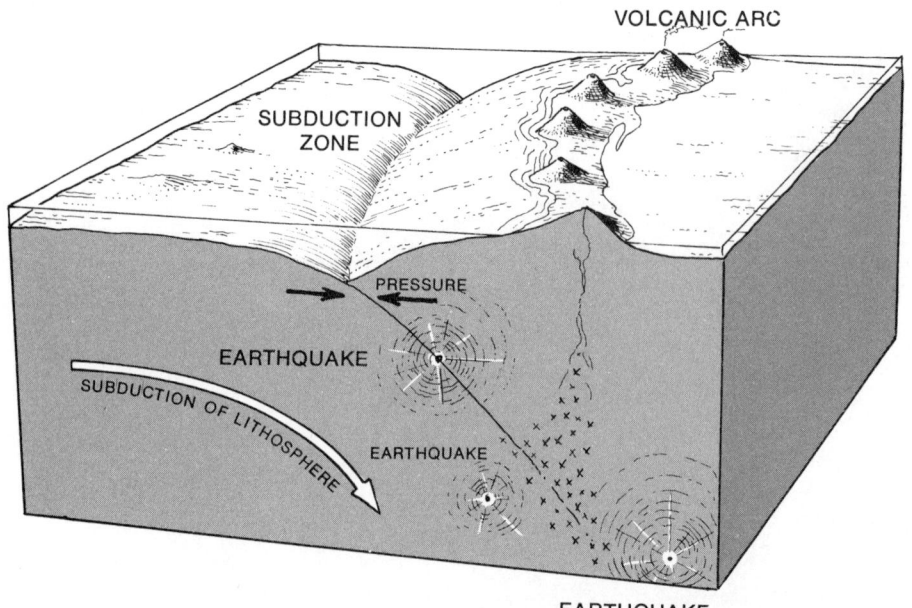

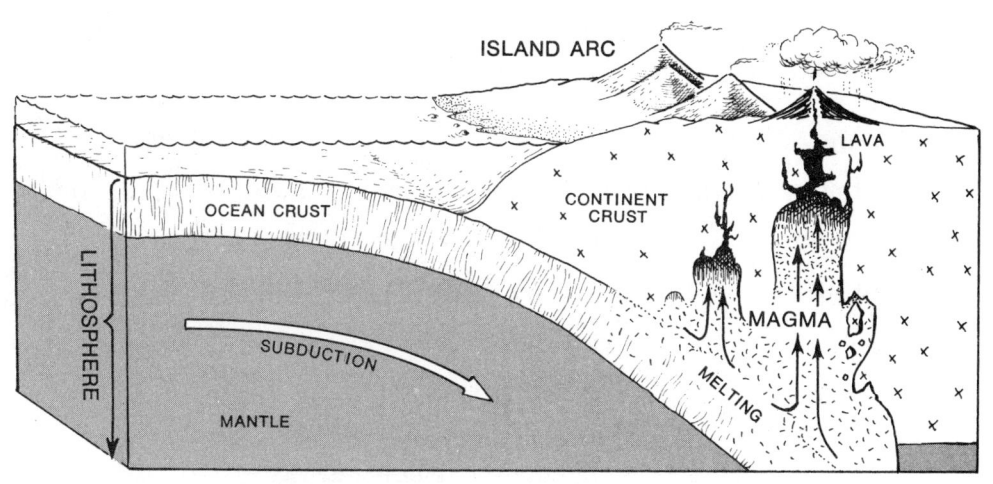

Island arcs developed from the magma that formed and erupted above subduction zones.

the oceans was related to subduction zones. That is, part of a slab of lithosphere melts as it sinks. That melting then produces hot magmas that, being liquid and therefore lighter, rise through the overriding plate, along fractures, and to the surface. There the magmas erupt and form a chain, or arc, of volcanoes that build up from the ocean floor.

In addition to magmas that erupted over subduction zones, there were large amounts of magma that never reached the surface. That magma cooled in the crust as great pods, called "plutons," which formed very coarse-grained rock. Eventually, over millions of years, pressures in the crust, some possibly from the continual plate movement, forced enormous blocks of that coarse-grained rock and other crustal rock to the surface. The result was the development of huge mountain ranges, such as the Sierra Nevadas in Cali-

Molten rock that formed in subduction zones
from partial melting of ocean rock
has contributed to the building of continents
in the form of large mountain ranges.

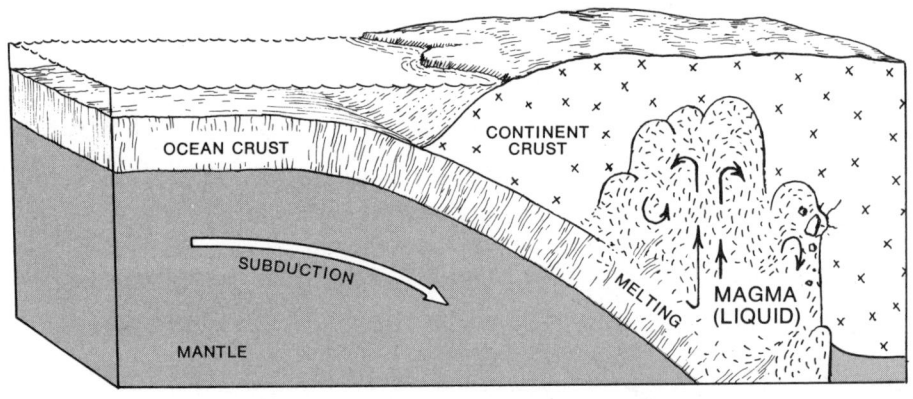

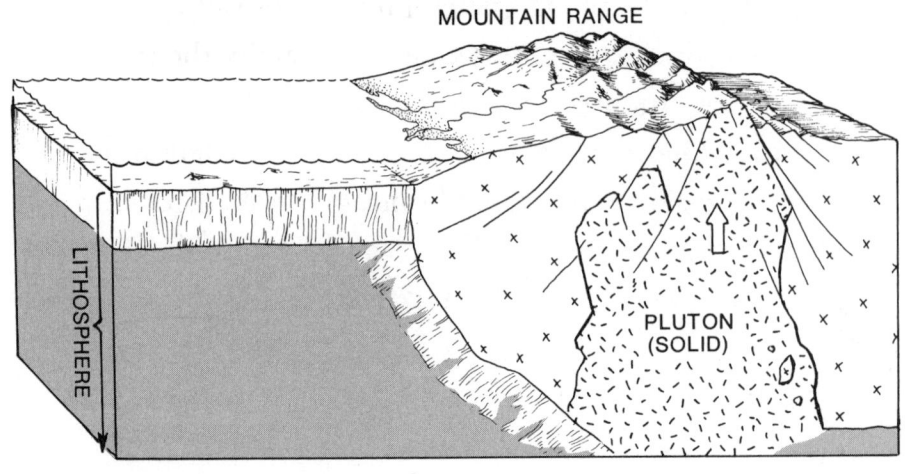

The Sierra Nevadas in California
are made largely of coarse-grained granitic rock—
magma that cooled beneath the surface
and later uplifted as enormous blocks.
W. C. Mendenhall; United States Geological Survey

fornia. In fact, many coastal ranges are thought by scientists to mark the sites of former subduction zones.

The rock of island arcs and mountain ranges that formed above subduction zones are usually the types known as "andesitic" or "granitic." Both differ in chemical composition from the basalt of the ocean crust. Namely, the andesitic and granitic rocks are richer in the elements silicon, potassium, and sodium, and poorer in the elements iron and magnesium.

These andesitic and granitic rocks in mountain ranges and island arcs represent another form of the Earth recycling itself. Scientifically, they are viewed as continental rocks that have been melted, or "sweated," out of the ocean crust in subduction zones. That is, as mentioned earlier, part of the sinking basaltic crust melts during subduction. But because only part of the basaltic rock melts, the melt produced has andesitic or granitic chemistry. That partial melt is lighter, or less dense than rock, and rises as hot magma high above the subduction zones, either near or on the surface. There it cools and becomes part of the continental crust. In this fashion, oceanic material gives "birth" to continental rock.

Not all of the Earth's mountain building has been related to the formation of magmas. The plate-tectonics concept also explains mountain building in areas where no significant volcanism has occurred. In these places the leading edges of two plates with continental crust met head on. Because of the buoyancy of the continents, neither plate sank beneath the other. Instead, great pushing forces developed between the two plates, and the continental crusts buckled into huge belts of folded mountains. The

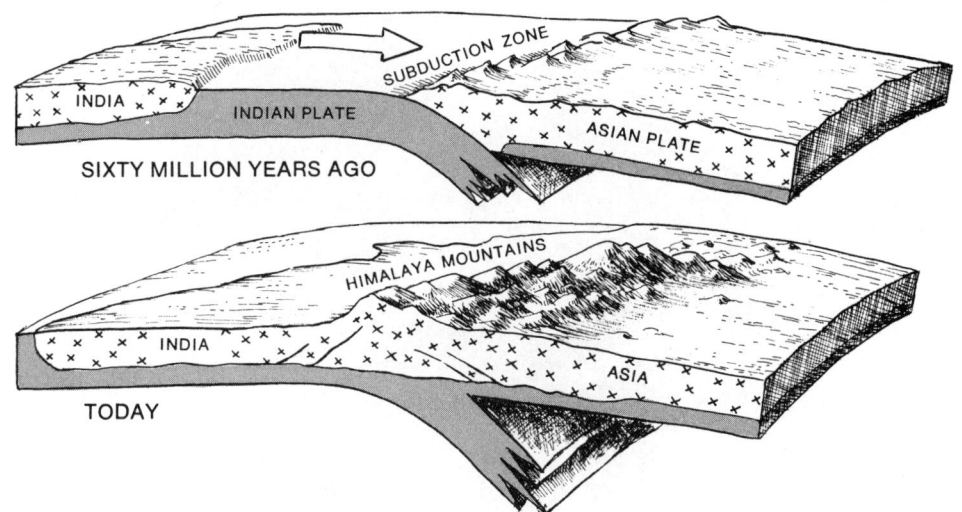

When two plates carrying continental crust collided, huge mountain ranges formed.

Himalayan Mountains, the highest in the world, are examples of mountains thought to be produced by the meeting of two plates of continental crust.

Through the model of plate tectonics, scientists are able to unravel the history of plate motion and reconstruct the surface of the Earth before the continents drifted. They believe that about 225 million years ago at the beginning of the Mesozoic geologic era, nearly all the world's landmass formed a supercontinent, which they give Wegener's name of Pangaea. At that time, North America, South America, and Africa were neatly fitted together, and both

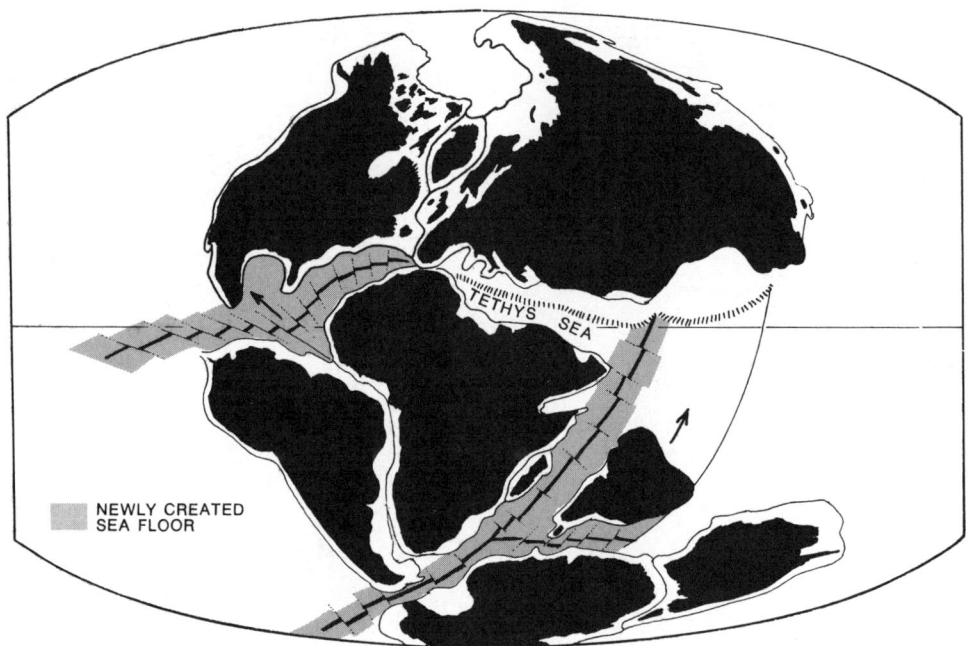

Here is how the Earth looked 180 million years ago or shortly after the continents began to break apart.

India and Australia were attached to the Antarctican continent. Between Africa and Eurasia was the Tethys Sea.

The time of initial breakup of the supercontinent is estimated to be about 200 million years ago. That event was marked by the opening of the North Atlantic Ocean as a plate "carrying" North America broke away from the African and South American plates. Left between them was a midocean ridge

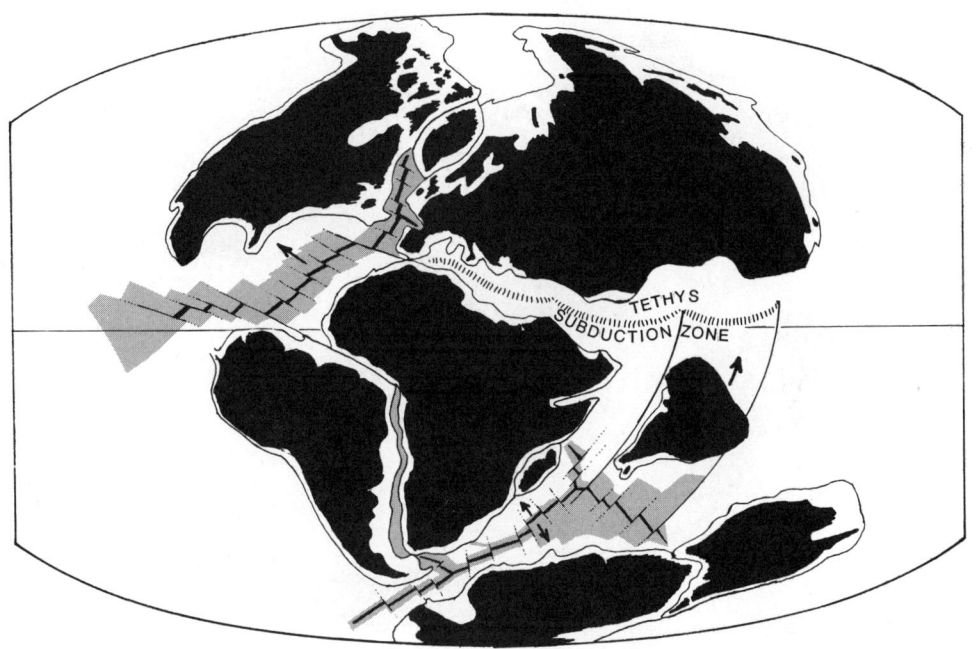

Earth, 140 million years ago

where new ocean crust was added. Another ocean ridge developed between Africa and Antarctica, and India broke away as a separate plate.

About 140 million years ago the ocean ridge between Africa and North America extended northward and separated the North American plate from the Eurasian plate. Both the African and Indian plates moved northward, closing the Tethys Sea. The African plate was being "consumed" at its northern

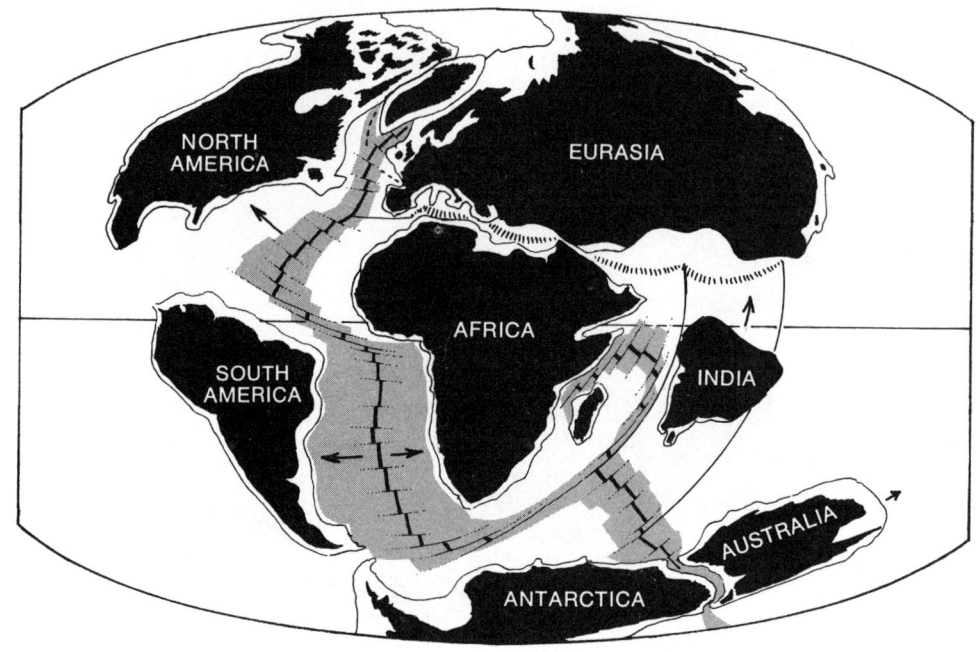

Earth, sixty million years ago

end in the Tethys trench, or subduction zone, and India approached Eurasia.

Sometime afterward, the South Atlantic Ocean opened due to further spreading along the now-called mid-Atlantic ridge between the South American and African plates. The western margin of North America overrode part of the Pacific plate, at which time coastal mountains developed, probably as an island-arc system. By about 60 million years ago, the

South Atlantic Ocean was extensive in size, the Australian plate had parted from Antarctica, and Madagascar broke away from Africa. The African plate had moved far enough northward to eliminate the Tethys Sea entirely.

Throughout the following 60 million years, plates drifted to their present positions. The North American and Eurasian plates completely separated, and the mid-Atlantic ridge extended northward to the Arctic. India plowed into the Eurasian plate, and the meeting of the two continental plates caused massive buckling of crust and formation of the Himalayas. Continued crustal spreading in the South Atlantic moved the South American plate northward to meet North America and pushed its western margin over an oceanic plate that was moving eastward from the East Pacific ridge. This collision created the Peru-Chile trench, or subduction zone, and the origin of the Andes Mountains is related to it. Northward movement of the Australian plate and westward movement of the Pacific plate produced a number of island-arc systems that now border the Pacific Ocean—in the so-called ring of fire.

It took approximately 200 million years—from

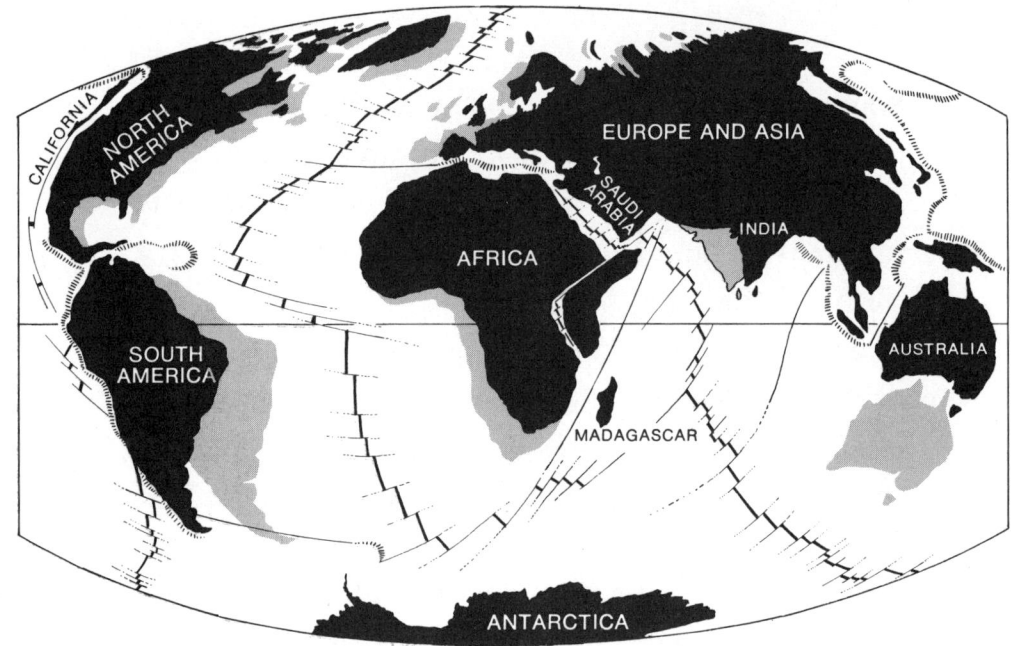

Earth, fifty million years *from now*:
note western North America and eastern Africa.
(Gray is present location.)

the time of the age of the dinosaurs—for the supercontinent to break up and form the Earth's surface as we see it today. Moreover, the plate-tectonics concept states that the plates are still moving. About 50 million years from now, the Earth's surface will look greatly different from the way it does today. Some of the most notable changes will be that a slice of North America that includes western California and Mexico and a slice of eastern Africa will have broken off from their respective continents. Each will have moved a great distance northward. Also, the Red Sea, located between Saudi Arabia and Africa, will be larger due to the continued drifting of Arabia away from Africa, and Australia will have moved farther north.

4

SCIENTIFIC EVIDENCE

The model describing our planet as having an outer shell of moving plates has proven to be a revolutionary concept in earth science. Although the groundwork for the idea of continental drift was laid early in this century, it did not develop into a concept of plate motion that the earth-science community

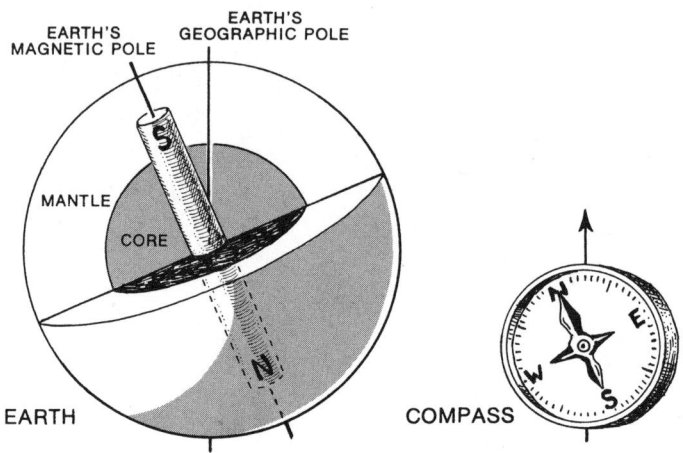

The Earth acts as a magnet.

found acceptable until the late 1960's. Why should acceptance have taken so long? It was known back in Wegener's time that fossils in South America and Africa suggested that those two continents were once a single landmass. It was also long obvious that their coastlines fit together like a jigsaw puzzle. What suddenly gave merit to what had seemed like an impossible idea?

Probably the one scientific accomplishment that proved to be the turning point was the determination of the magnetic properties of the basaltic rock forming the ocean crust.

That the Earth acts as a large magnet is ancient knowledge. It has a magnetic axis that is almost in line with the axis it rotates on. The present arrangement of the Earth's magnetic field is such that the north geographic pole behaves as the south pole of a magnet. Because the unlike poles of a magnet, north and south, attract each other, the north pole of a compass points to the south pole of the magnetic earth, the north geographic pole.

It has also long been known that many types of rocks contain minerals that became weakly magnetized as they cooled from magma. Rocks that formed from molten material are called "igneous." They preserve in themselves the direction of the Earth's

Some minerals in cooling lava flows acquired properties that indicate the direction of the Earth's magnetic field at that time.

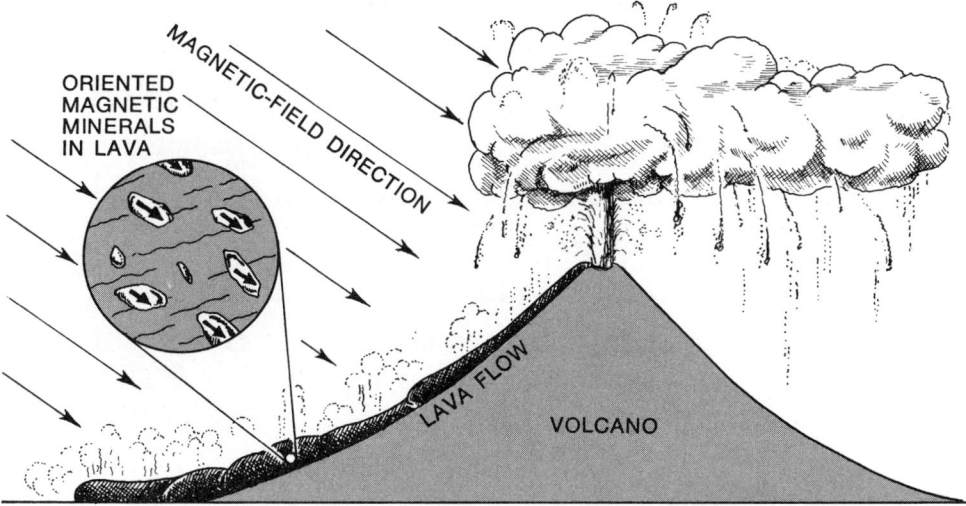

magnetic field at the time of their formation. That is, the magnetic properties of a rock that forms today from the magma erupting from a volcano on Hawaii will record that the Earth's north geographic pole behaves like the south pole of a magnet.

Scientists were surprised then, when they learned from the magnetic properties of many igneous rocks that formed millions of years ago that the Earth's north geographic pole had sometimes acted like the north pole of magnet. The north pole of a compass would have pointed to the Earth's south pole.

Through methods developed by scientists for determining the ages of igneous rocks, a geologic time scale was established for rocks on land. This scale showed the times in the geologic past when the Earth's magnetic field was normal, or as it is today, and when it was reversed. It illustrated that sometimes several hundred thousands of years passed before there was a change in the magnetic field. But the different time periods were not equal; some periods of normal magnetism lasted much longer than others.

In the late 1950's and early 1960's, the magnetic properties of the igneous rocks of the ocean crust (basaltic rocks) were determined by magnetometers on ships and airplanes. In the ocean basalt, too, magnetic reversals were observed. When the data for the ocean floor were plotted on maps, "magnetic stripes" that ran parallel to the ocean ridges showed

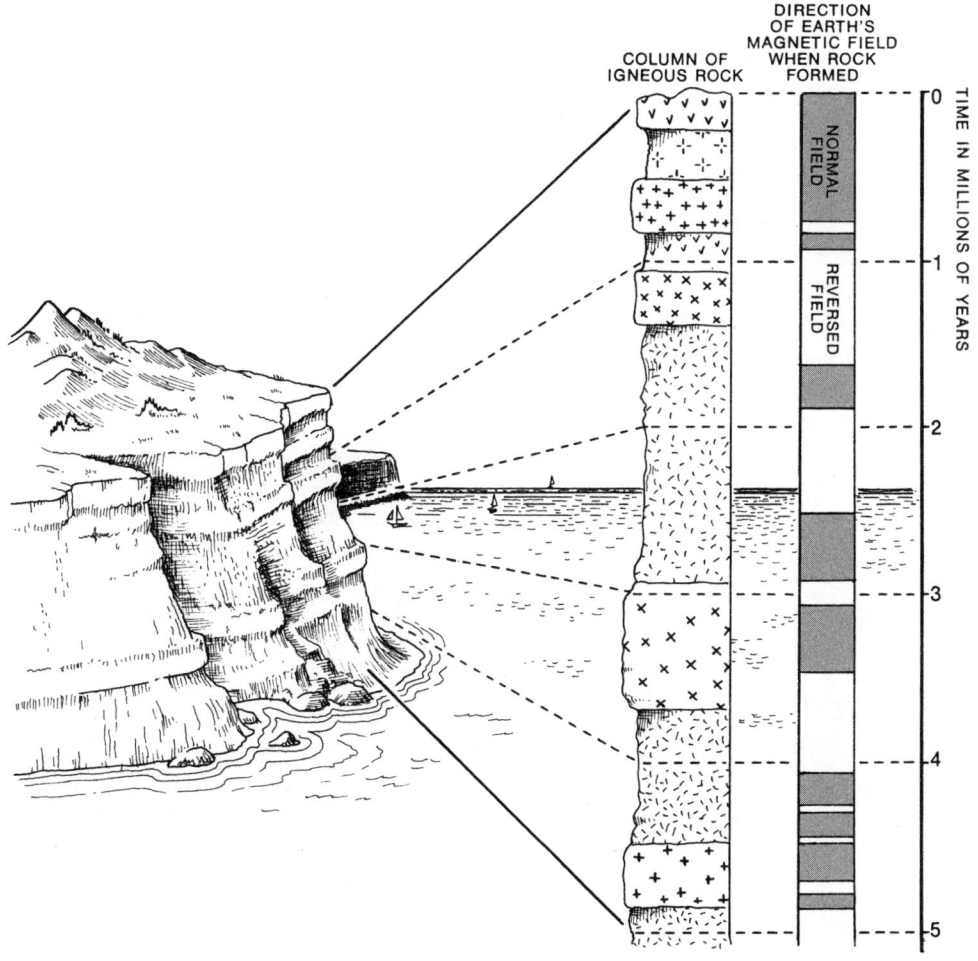

A column of lava flows, for which the ages are known, can be used to make a magnetic-reversals time scale.

up. On each side of an ocean ridge was basaltic crust having stripes of normal magnetic properties next to stripes of reversed magnetic properties. Furthermore, the pattern of alternating magnetic stripes on one side of the ridge was a mirror image of the pattern on the other.

When scientists compared those stripes to the geologic time scale determined for igneous rocks on continents, they found that the farther away ocean crust is from a ridge, the older it is. They interpreted this finding to mean that the ocean crust was indeed

The mirroring magnetic stripes on the ocean floors
show changes in the magnetic field of the Earth
throughout geologic time;
the farthest from the ridge are the oldest.

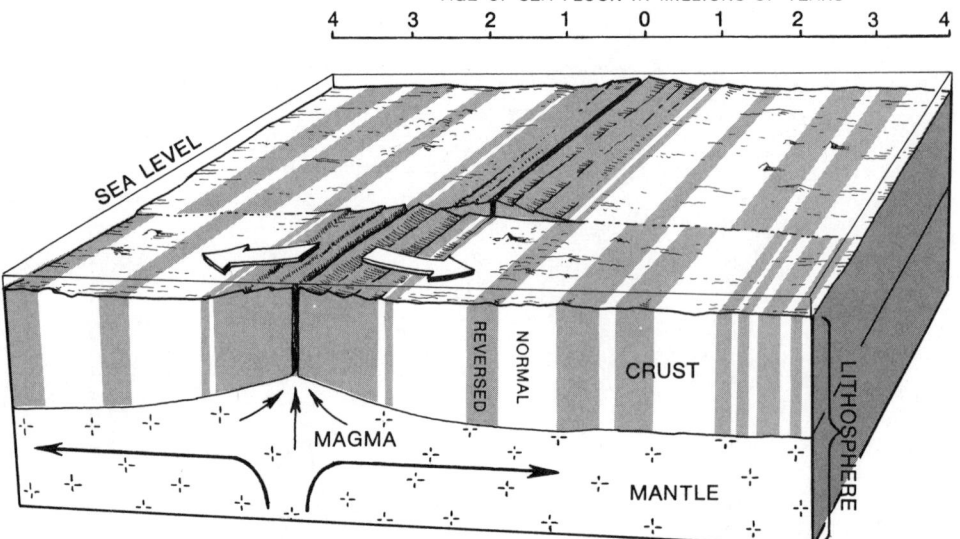

the drilling ship *Glomar Challenger*
Deep Sea Drilling Project

spreading away from its source—the ocean ridges. The magnetic stripes of the ocean crust recorded the development of ocean floors much the way tree rings record the age of a tree.

Additional scientific data to support the idea of a spreading sea floor became available in 1968. In that year a special investigation was started by the National Science Foundation, and it still goes on today. This project uses a large ship that has a drilling derrick straddling the center. The ship is the research vessel *Glomar Challenger,* and the investigation is called the Deep Sea Drilling Project. As

Drillers aboard the *Glomar Challenger* string pipe to the ocean floor.
R. V. Fodor

the name of the project implies, its goal is to drill the ocean floor and recover samples for study.

From the derrick on the *Challenger,* thousands of meters of drilling pipe, the same as that used for oil-well drilling on land, can be sent down like spaghetti

A core barrel of rock drilled from the Pacific Ocean floor comes up through the pipe on the *Glomar Challenger*.
R. V. Fodor

string to the ocean floor. This drilling pipe is capable of recovering cores of any material drilled. After drilling and coring at selected depths in the ocean floor, the material is brought to the surface and studied by scientists.

Technicians carry a core of ocean-floor rock
to a laboratory aboard ship.
R. V. Fodor

Within months of the start of the Deep Sea Drilling Project, samples of the basalt and sediments (largely clay, mud, and limestone) on the sea floors confirmed sea-floor spreading. These samples showed that the oldest material on the ocean floor was farth-

Scientists in the lab examine the material from the ocean floor.
R. V. Fodor

est away from the ocean ridges. By determining the ages of certain basaltic rocks, and by studying the fossils in the sediments above the basalt, scientists calculated the dates of major geologic events in the Earth's history. For example, they determined that the South Atlantic Ocean began to open about 120 million years ago. By age dating rock samples, they also calculated how fast the ocean floor spreads, which was shown to be from about one to six centimeters per year, depending on the plate and its location.

The *Glomar Challenger* has continued to drill in the oceans of the world. Drilling operations at over 450 sites have recovered thousands of cores of sediment and igneous rock that make up the ocean floors. Scientific determinations of the types and ages of sediments, the fossils within, and the igneous rocks provide a steady stream of new information about plate tectonics.

There has been ample evidence found on land, too, showing that continents once were joined together. Rock-dating studies in Africa showed that in the countries of Ghana and Ivory Coast in western Africa, there are two distinct geologic provinces, one 2000 million years old and the other 600 million years old. That discovery inspired scientists who hoped either to prove or disprove continental drift to try to locate the same geologic boundary across the South Atlantic Ocean in the rocks of Brazil. Just

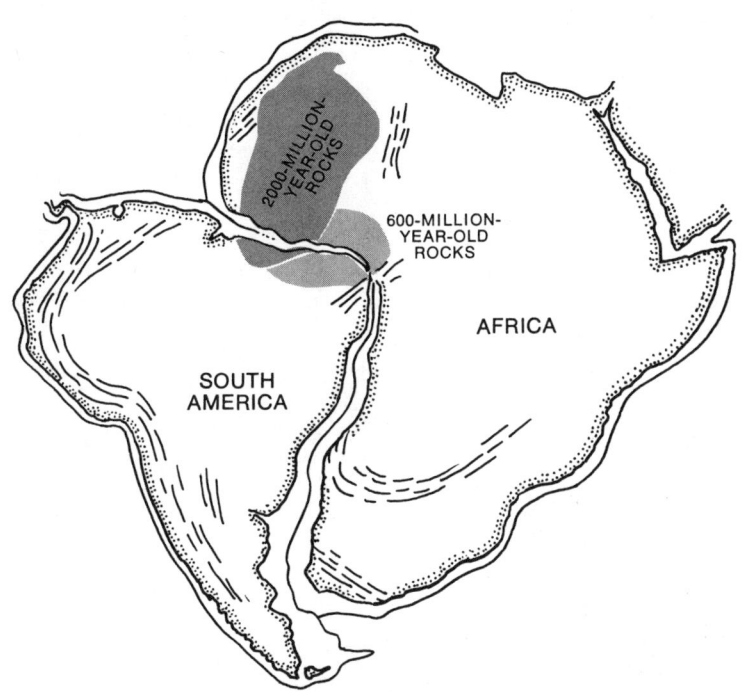

Similar rock ages and types on South America and Africa indicate that these continents were once joined as a larger landmass.

as predicted by many scientists, the dating of rocks from Brazil did show the same geologic provinces that are present in Africa. These identical regions on opposite sides of the Atlantic Ocean could only mean that South America had indeed been connected to Africa.

Other similarities among the geologic structures and rock types on all the continents have also been

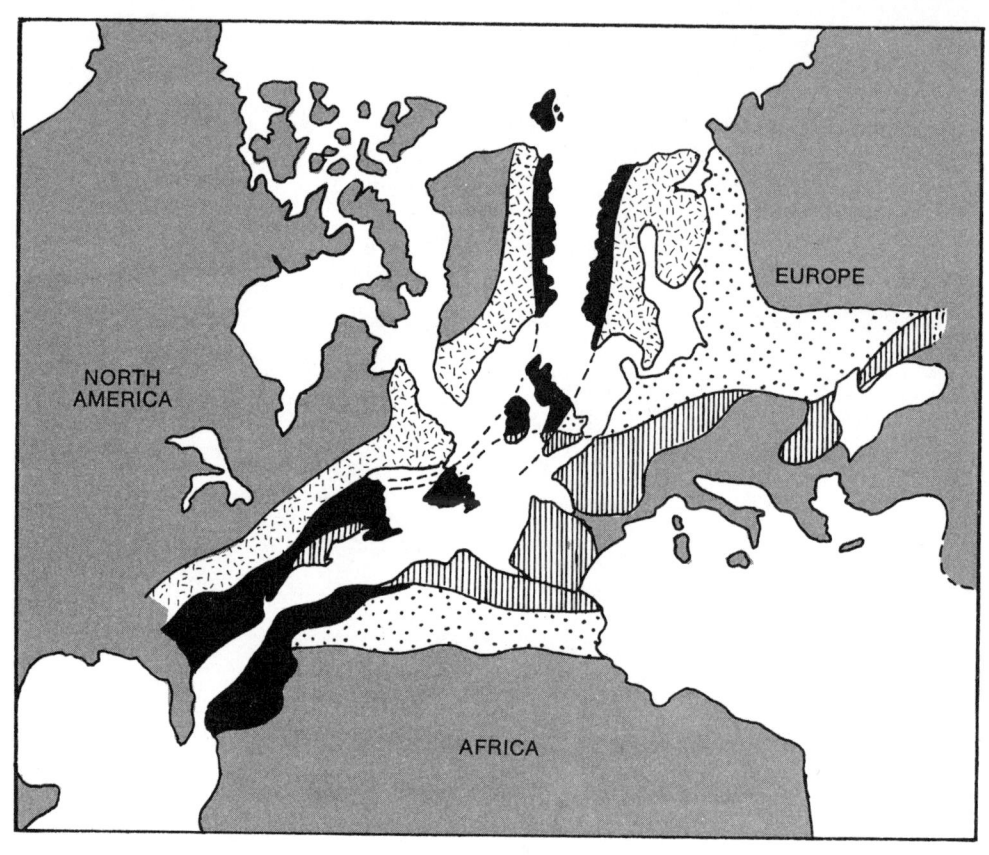

Similar geology found on the margins of North America, Europe, and Africa indicate that they were once joined.

observed, and then provide further evidence of a one-time supercontinent. Throughout eastern North America, western Europe, and northwest Africa are geologic features that neatly match up when the continents are reconstructed as one landmass. Furthermore, the same type of geologic matching occurs throughout southern Africa, Australia, Antarctica, and Madagascar. All of this matching of geology across oceans is far too impressive to be shrugged off as merely coincidence. Hence, an overwhelming number of scientists feel there is solid evidence supporting the concept of plate tectonics.

5

APPLICATIONS IN DAILY LIFE

Understanding the concept of plate tectonics has proved to be of practical as well as theoretical use. For example, scientists now know much more about the minerals and petroleum that formed due to geologic processes associated with plate motion.

Some important and useful minerals that are

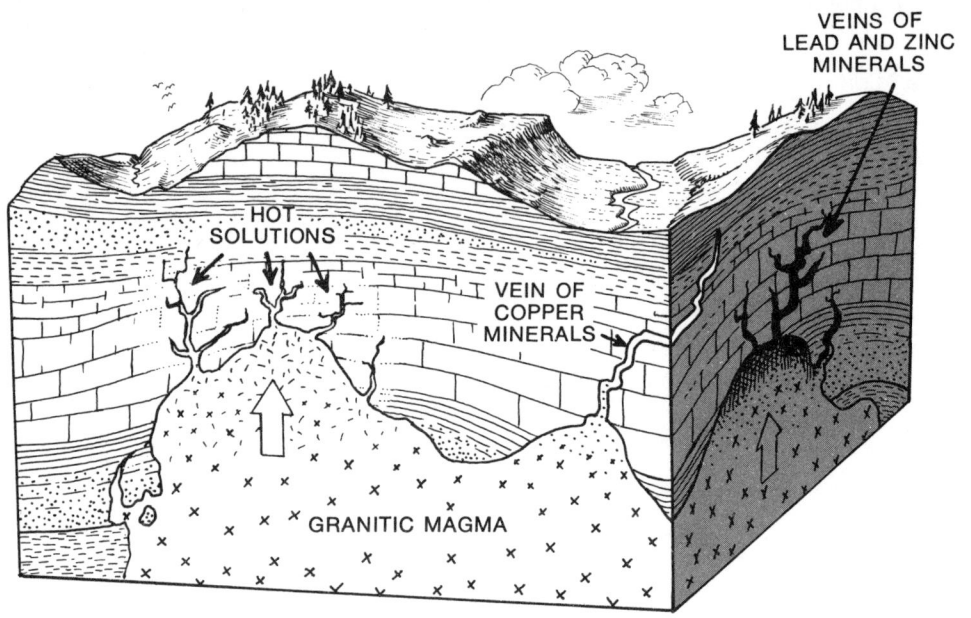

Many of the Earth's valuable ore deposits formed from hot solutions associated with molten rock.

mined on the continents are those that formed from hot liquids, or solutions, that once moved through parts of the crust. Deposits of minerals that formed from such solutions are referred to as "hydrothermal mineral deposits." Many of these deposits are rich in metals such as copper, iron, lead, zinc, and even gold, most of which we use everyday. For example, they compose the airplanes, cars, and bicycles that we travel on, and the wires that bring electricity and telephone calls into our homes.

Geologists have noted that many hydrothermal

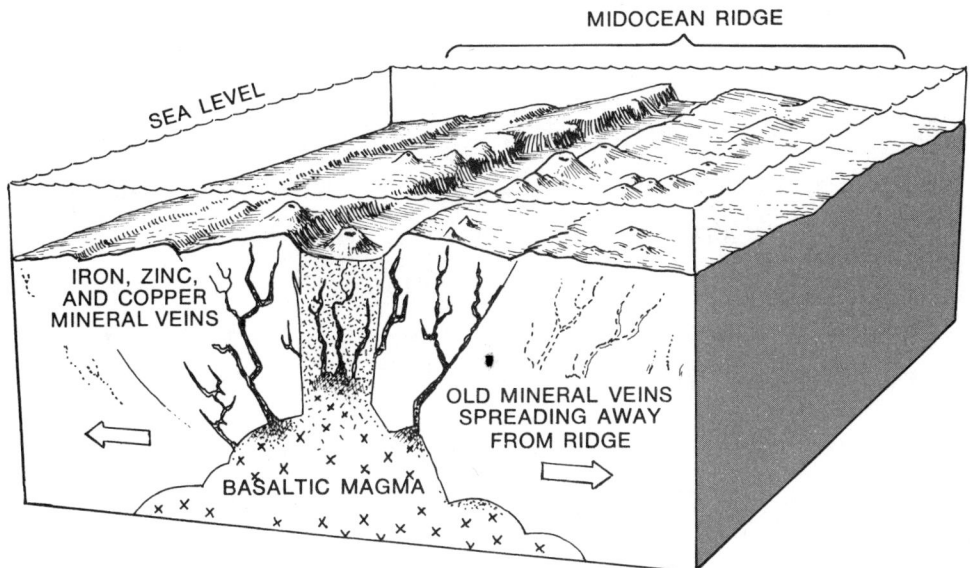

Mineral deposits formed on midocean ridges.

deposits are in areas near plate boundaries at subduction zones. They believe that the solutions that deposited those minerals formed when magmas were made by the melting of sinking plates of ocean crust. Examples of important mineral deposits related to such plate boundaries are found in Japan, the Philippines, and the mountain ranges along the west coasts of North and South America.

Plate margins where lithosphere is being created, as at midocean ridges, have also been important in forming hydrothermal deposits. In fact, the formation of mineral deposits is known to be going on now at the bottom of the Red Sea. There the Eurasian plate is slowly separating from the African plate, and a new ocean ridge is forming. Scientists have discovered deposits rich in iron, zinc, and copper in sediments at about 2000 meters of water depth.

The floor of the Red Sea, where volcanic activity and mineral formation are taking place.
D. A. Ross

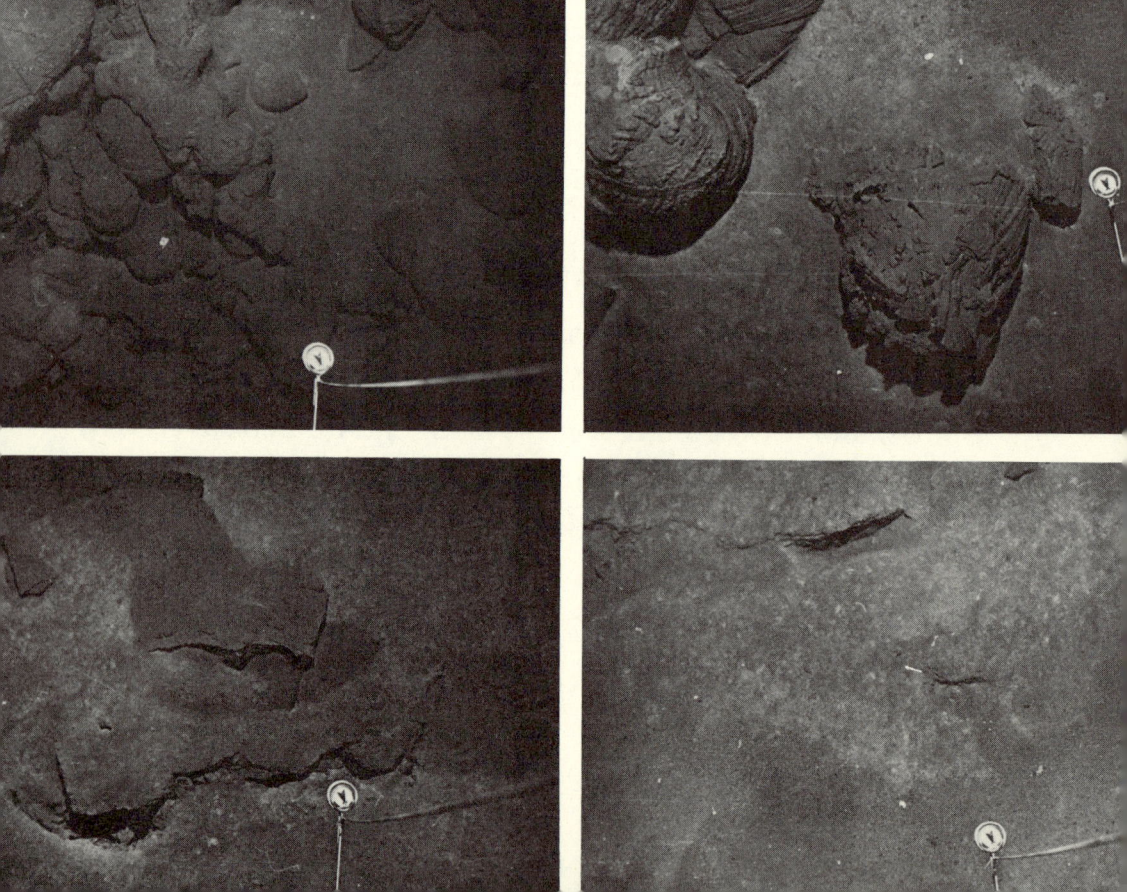

Associated with the deposits are salty solutions rich in the same metals. These solutions are believed to be depositing the minerals in that underwater region.

At this time, it is not known exactly how great a mineral supply will be found along the Earth's 65,000-kilometer chain of ocean ridge. However, one mineral-rich island in the Mediterranean Sea provides geologists with a good idea of what may be present on certain parts of the ridge system. The island is Cyprus, and it has been mined for its rich deposits of copper since Roman times. Studies of Cyprus show that it has many geologic features similar to those of ocean crust. In fact, geologists believe that the island represents a portion of ocean crust that was forced above sea level long ago by plate movements.

Scientific examinations of active portions of the ridge system have also shown sediments rich in nickel, chromium, cobalt, and uranium. But how long the extraction of any of these metals from the ocean ridges will take is something no one really knows. The reason is that there are problems of *how* to recover the mineral deposits and in deciding *who* is entitled to them.

Many years will be needed to develop the necessary equipment, or technology, to mine the deposits of ocean ridges—and to do so at a profit. Also, organizations like the United Nations must decide who owns the portions of oceans that are far from land and to whom do the minerals belong. Furthermore, scientists and engineers must consider what effects

one way that deep-ocean mining may be done

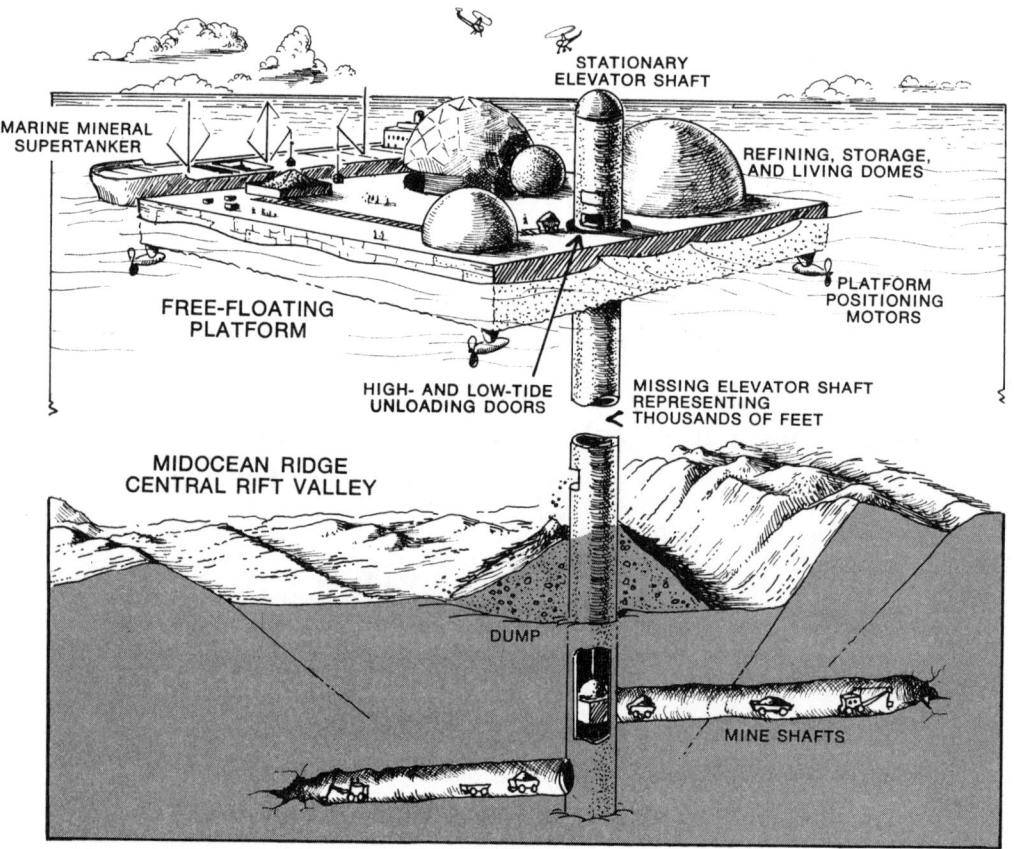

mining the ocean ridges will have on the environment of the seas. Operations must be planned so that little disturbance, if any, is brought to sea life and food chains, and certainly there should be no polluting of the water. No longer can people use the Earth without considering the possible harm they may do.

Nevertheless, mining the ocean ridges is of great importance to the world's population. Clearly the mineral deposits on land will not last forever, no matter how wisely we try to conserve the supply.

Petroleum and gas deposits also developed in certain geologic environments associated with the movement of plates. These products are essential for our transportation and heating, and petroleum is even used for making some of the clothes we wear. The formation of oil and gas required (1) a large supply of the dead remains of plants and animals, called "organic" material; (2) a natural reservoir, or burial ground, to contain the remains; and (3) a trap to retain the material. Also, to preserve the organic matter, the reservoirs must have been low in oxygen content; too much air in water will destroy organic matter.

Oftentimes in the geologic past, all of these conditions were met in the trenches associated with island arcs and continental margins. The trenches caught the sediments and organic matter of the oceans and those washed in from land. Oxygen cir-

The oil that formed in subduction-zone trenches is being drilled today.

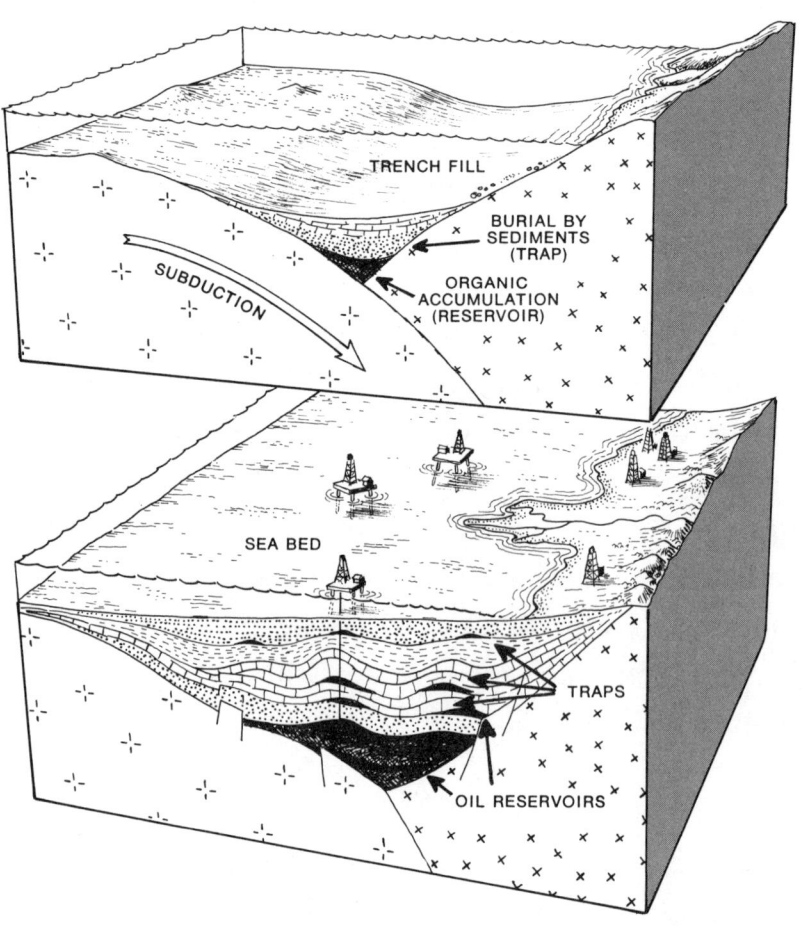

culation in them was low enough to keep from destroying the organic material. And the continual addition of sediments from the ocean water buried the organic matter. Those sediments later served as traps for petroleum that formed from the organic

Drilling rigs like this one are used by oil companies to help find more oil in ocean-floor rocks.
Phillips Petroleum Company

matter. Many of the rocks in the Earth's former trenches are now providing the oil and gas in use today.

Excellent conditions for oil formation also occurred when continents first began to rift, or open. The rifting resulted in the formation of small seas blocked by continents on each side with poor oxygen circulation. Consequently, organic material that ac-

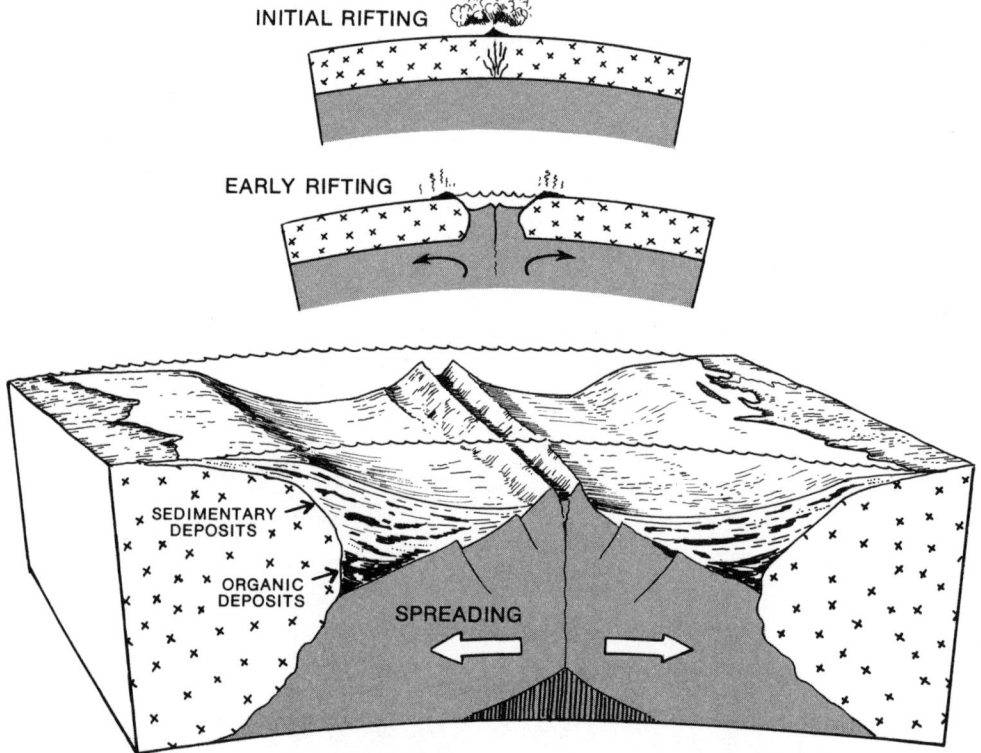

Organic material accumulated to form oil when oceans like the Atlantic first opened.

cumulated on the sea floors was preserved. Later the organic material became deeply buried by sediments as the continents continued to rift and the seas became the oceans we know today. Eventually petroleum and gas were formed in those regions that were once the floors of small seas.

Largely due to the knowledge of plate tectonics, more and more oil and gas are being recovered from the rocks of the ocean floors. But our excessive use of these resources means we must continually search the oceans for more. Thus, the world's oil and gas deposits are rapidly being depleted.

The action of plate tectonics can be harmful to people, too. A most important example is an earthquake. Anywhere there is contact between two moving plates, there is likely to be friction and sudden crustal movements—or earthquakes. And the results of earthquakes cost thousands of lives and millions of dollars in property damage each year.

The greatest movements in the Earth's crust generally occur along major plate boundaries, such as the San Andreas Fault. That fault runs almost the entire length of California, and movements there have been measured at up to six meters during one

The San Andreas Fault (narrow valley in center) runs 1000 kilometers through California, marking a plate boundary.
R. E. Wallace; United States Geological Survey

quake. The cause of these quakes is the slow but persistent northward movement of the western portion of California. In addition to the San Andreas Fault, California is riddled with dozens of other faults. Although less active, these smaller faults are

The lines on this map of California represent faults, or fractures, in the Earth's crust.

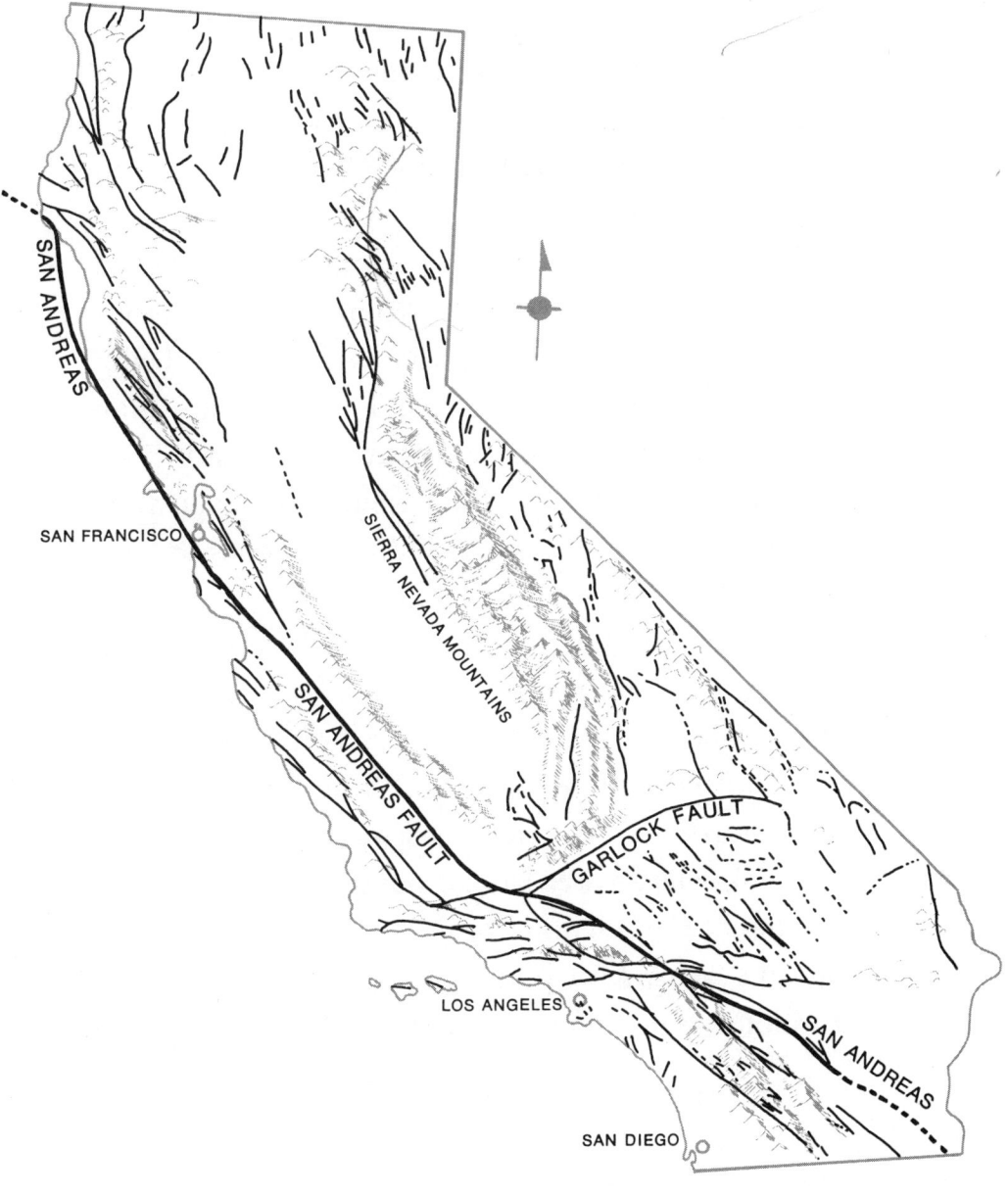

related to plate motion, too, and are the sites of numerous earthquakes in many highly populated areas.

The Andes Mountains also have been subjected to many powerful and devastating earthquakes because part of the Pacific plate is sinking beneath the South American plate.

Another action of plate tectonics that can be harmful is volcanism. Such geologic activity is related to magmas rising to the surface after being formed near subduction zones. These magmas may erupt on populated islands that form part of an island-arc chain, such as Japan. Similarly, volcanism occurs on the surface over subduction zones at continental margins. One example is the volcanic activity in densely populated Central America.

Thus, the concept of plate tectonics plays both a positive and negative role in our daily lives. But must we experience any danger at all from the movement of the Earth's plates? Geologists are now working to help make the answer to that question *no*.

Some of the scientific projects under way include warning systems for both earthquakes and volcanic eruptions. For example, scientists now can identify small changes in how sound waves and electric current pass through the crust before some earthquakes occur. They also can detect tilting of the ground that sometimes signals earthquakes and eruptions.

Paricutín Volcano erupted in a Mexican cornfield in 1950. Its origin is related to a trench and subduction zone that borders Central America.
F. O. Jones; United States Geological Survey

Another project planned is to lubricate areas of the crust known to have major earthquakes. This process involves forcing water down into earthquake zones to help the crust move; that way, the move-

A geologist sets up a tiltmeter to help study
the Earth's movement near the San Andreas Fault.
United States Geological Survey

ment will be controlled and not take residents of those areas by surprise. Engineers, too, are working to construct stronger buildings so that they can survive earthquakes. For some of us, however, the answer may be not to live in areas of the world threatened by earthquakes and volcanoes.

There is still much to learn about the concept of plate tectonics and the behavior of our living planet. Although scientists can help make living with the dangers presented by an earth in motion easier, can they ever really win a battle against them? That is certainly a challenge. Yet, with steady effort, the results should clearly help us achieve better harmony between life on earth and an earth that lives.

INDEX

indicates illustration

Age dating, 70-71*
Andes Mountains, 24*, 55, 88
Andesitic rock, 22*, 40-50
Asthenosphere, 23*

Basalt rock, 22*, 49, 50, 60, 63*-64, 68-69

Continental drift, 11-14, 12*, 16, 38, 42, 59
Convection currents, 15*, 16*, 38*, 39
Core, 21, 23*
Crust, 21-23, 22*; composition of, 22*, 49; of continents, 21-22*, 43, 50; of

ocean, 21-22*, 40*, 43, 50, 60, 62-64*, 79, 80

Deep Sea Drilling Project, 65*-70, 66*, 67*, 68*, 69*

Earthquakes, 24-25, 85-91, 86*, 87*; at midocean ridges, 29*-30; at island arcs, 34*-35; at plate boundaries, 46*, 85-88, 86*, 87*; warning signals, 88-91

Faults, 85-88, 86*, 87*

Gas. *See* Petroleum
Glomar Challenger, 65*-70, 66*, 67*, 68*, 69*
Gondwana Series, 13, 14*
Gondwanaland, 9
Granitic rock, 22*, 49-50

Heat currents. *See* Convection currents.
H.M.S. Challenger, 26
Holmes, Arthur, 14-16, 39

Igneous rock, 61*-62, 70
Island arcs, 33*-34*, 35, 46-47*, 49, 50, 55, 88

Lithosphere, 22*-23, 39-43, 40*, 41*, 42*, 47*, 77; melting of, 47-50, 77

Magma, 39-40*, 47*, 48*, 50, 61, 88
Magnetic properties, of Earth, 60*-62, 61*; of crust, 63*-65, 64*
Mantle, 21-23*, 22*, 39, 40*, 41*
Mesosphere, 23*
Mid-Atlantic ridge, 28*, 31*, 55
Midocean ridges, 28*-32, 29*, 30*, 31*, 38*-40*, 42-45*, 44*, 64*, 65, 69, 77*-79
Mineral deposits, 75-80, 76*, 77*, 80*
Mining, 80*-81
Mountain building, 48*-51*, 49*

Oil. *See* Petroleum.

Pangaea, 11, 12*, 51
Peridotite rock, 21
Petroleum, 81-85, 82*, 83*, 84*
Plate margins, 43*-46, 44*, 45*, 77
Plate tectonics, definition of, 42-43

94

Plates, of lithosphere, 42*-45*, 43*, 44*, 52*-56*, 53*, 54*
Plutons, 47*-48*

Ring of fire, 25*, 33*, 55

San Andreas Fault, 85-87*, 86*, 90
Sea-floor spreading, 37-41*, 38*, 40*, 65, 68
Seamounts, 32*, 33
Seismic waves, 20-21
Seismograph, 20*
Sierra Nevadas, 24*, 48-49*
Subduction zones, 41*-42, 44*-47*, 45*, 46*, 49, 50, 51*, 82*, 88

Submarines, 27*
Submersibles, 27*

Time scales, geologic, 62-64*, 63*
Trenches, ocean-floor, 33*, 34*-35*, 41*, 42, 43, 82*-84*

Volcanic islands, 31*-34*, 32*, 33*
Volcanism, 24, 30, 88 ,89*; at midocean ridges, 30-31, 39; at plate margins, 46; warning signals, 88-89

Wegener, Alfred, 10-15, 38, 51, 60

About the Author

Ronald V. Fodor was born in Cleveland, Ohio, and received a B.S. from Ohio University. He continued his geologic studies at Arizona State University and the University of New Mexico where he earned an M.S. and a Ph.D., respectively. Dr. Fodor worked as a research scientist at the University of New Mexico for six years, and is currently on the geology faculty at North Carolina State University. He has published extensively in scientific journals and has been to sea twice on the *Glomar Challenger,* the research vessel responsible for obtaining much of the information on plate tectonics.

Earth in Motion is Dr. Fodor's third book for children. At present he lives with his wife and two children in Raleigh, North Carolina.

About the Illustrator

John C. Holden is a geologist and science illustrator who lives in Winthrop, Washington. As a scientist, he has published dozens of articles, with emphasis on plate tectonics. His drawings have appeared in numerous scientific publications, including *Scientific American.*